## DATE DUE

| | | | |
|---|---|---|---|
| | | | |
| | | | |
| | | | |
| | | | |
| | | | |
| | | | |
| | | | |
| | | | |
| | | | |
| | | | |
| | | | |
| | | | |
| | | | |
| | | | |
| | | | |
| | | | |
| | | | |

DEMCO 38-296

# QUALITY PERFORMANCE

# QUALITY PERFORMANCE

**How to Implement**

> **Quality Awareness**
> **Statistical Process Control**
> **Task Teams**
> **Statistical Quality Control**

**For Continuous Improvement**
**in Your Organization**

**By Nancy Sue Mitchell**

**QP Publishing, Pittsburgh, Pennsylvania**

# RMANCE

## Quality Awareness
## Statistical Process Control
## Task Teams
## Statistical Quality Control

## For Continuous Improvement
## in Your Organization

## By Nancy Sue Mitchell

**Published by:**

**QP Publishing
Box 18281
Pittsburgh, PA  15236-0281  U.S.A.**

Library of Congress Cataloging in Publication Data - Card Number Preassigned is:
90-091657
Mitchell, Nancy Sue
QUALITY PERFORMANCE: How to Implement Quality Awareness, Statistical Process Control, Task Teams, and Statistical Quality Control for Continuous Improvement in Your Organization / by Nancy Sue Mitchell

CIP 90-091657
ISBN 0-9626692-5-3

I dedicate this, my first
book to three individuals:
First, to my Mom,
then to Matthew
and Joshua
(my two poodles).

# Quality :

**the thing remembered
long after the
price is forgotten.**

# CONTENTS

# CONTENTS CONTINUED

# CHAPTER 1

## LEADERSHIP

**Q**UALITY PERFORMANCE - every employer, employee, coworker, customer, and supplier *wants it.* What is it that everyone wants? Merchandise, services, information, and receipt of payment, in excellent condition, in a timely manner, at the lowest possible cost, *consistently* as we would want it for ourselves.

Quality in your products and service is today's way to achieve increased market share. You cannot afford to sort, test, or inspect to get it.

How do we achieve Quality Performance? The answer is similar to a body building commercial: *"If it came in a bottle, everyone would have it."* Unfortunately, it is not that simple. It takes work. Lots of it. But it does get easy. You will notice this transition as people work smarter, not harder. It is so much easier to prevent rather than to cure something. And any company can do it.

This book will give you step-by-step instructions on how to start a Quality Performance program if you are at ground zero. Or you can give your existing Quality Department ideas to generate more participation from employees, training in both statistical and problem solving tools, and flourish teams. These tools can benefit any size company, large or small. Programs can be modified to fit most any type of business: manufacturing; retail; or service industries. Each company has its own culture. Choose your approach to the improvement tactics for your organization.

One of the most important concepts in reaching your goals is the use of teamwork. It is the quality of your products, work performance, services to customers, and image in the marketplace that keeps you competitive in your business. Each employee plays an important part in the quality of what you sell. When you get everyone involved, contributing their expertise (teamwork), you can not help but succeed. Everyone wants to do a good job. Your people are your key to your success.

It is management's obligation to determine what is important for business survival and growth and to lead the team to those goals. This style, **PARTICIPATIVE MANAGEMENT**, eliminates the old style where managers had tight control of their respective functions. This new style delegates responsibility and authority downward. However, without Leadership, there can be no Management System. The system needs to be **management lead and customer driven.** The Quality Process translates into everyone working as a team and understanding his or her role as an individual in meeting the customer expectations every time.

It is extremely beneficial to supply everyone with training in Statistical and Problem Solving Tools (Chapter 4) so that everyone is speaking the same language. Statistics alone will not result in continuous improvement. Quality Performance will only be a buzz word if management, starting at the top, does not support it. This commitment includes **both** financial and physical obligations. Although the financial commitment need not be great, without both, the system is sure to fail. Employees, customers, and suppliers need to see that top management is committed to continuously improving outputs and inputs. Once management is fully supportive and involved, you will want to get the rest of the company, organization, group, or department involved. This may require overcoming unsatisfactory prior experiences with change programs and the belief that the Quality Program is just another form of cost control. This is not a *"Program of the Month"* system. Much energy will be required to tell and sell the many facets of the program.

## QUALITY STEERING COMMITTEE

To best lead and oversee your Quality Performance Program, you should have a Steering Committee of company or plant staff (**Figure 1-1**). This committee should have representation from every department and include guidance from the top boss. The committee chairperson need not be the President, Plant Manager or Store Manager. The Quality Performance Manager would be ideal to chair

---

# STEERING COMMITTEE

- PRESIDENT - OR - PLANT MANAGER - OR -
    STORE MANAGER
- VICE PRESIDENT OF QUALITY - OR -
    QUALITY ASSURANCE MANAGER

- QUALITY PERFORMANCE MANAGER
    * CHAIRPERSON *

- TECHNICAL MANAGER
- SAFETY MANAGER
- PRODUCTION MANAGER
- EMPLOYEE RELATIONS MANAGER
- FINANCE MANAGER
- ENGINEERING MANAGER
- MAINTENANCE MANAGER
- PLUS THE TRAINED FACILITATORS

---

FIGURE 1-1 :  QUALITY STEERING COMMITTEE

the committee since that person is keenly aware of quality and continually updated on various quality issues. The Quality Steering Committee:

1. Establishes clear requirements to objectively measure quality. Requirements are the expectations of your customers.

2. Presents an attitude to produce error free work. Do it right the first time, next time, and *every* time.

3. Sets targets to manage by prevention.

4. Identifies and prioritizes what is to be measured. As data is collected, have it displayed in a form meaningful to employees.

5. Sets guidelines for the improvement system.

6. Takes ownership and responsibility for quality.

## FACILITATORS

Have several employees in the role of Facilitators. A *Facilitator* is one who coaches, trains and is an internal consultant. With teams, a Facilitator gives responsibility to the team but remains accountable, is effective at motivating the teams, and can supply statistical and problem solving tools for productive meeting management and project maturity. Prerequisites for Facilitators are needing to have a genuine concern for quality improvement and have an *enthusiasm* for working with people.

Include the Facilitators in this Quality Steering Committee.  The Facilitators should have outside training in statistics (statistical process control and statistical quality control), teams, and problem solving tools.  This training is necessary to lead in the various activities of the program.  You want to train your key implementors.  Several companies have specialized training for Facilitators.  These can be found advertised in most quality type magazines.  You can select which curriculum is best for your organization.

The Facilitators can be full time or part time in the Quality Performance Department.  Depending how many you have, their time can be divided from 1/4 to 1/2 facilitating, and the rest in their primary job function (engineering, accounting, manufacturing, employee relations, or other).  By using experienced company employees as part time Facilitators, you have the benefit of professionals learning more about the company (plant, office, or store) to utilize in their main work.  Having at least one full time Facilitator helps to keep all the activities organized.

Initially, the Quality Steering Committee may be required to meet once a week to get the program organized and on track. Within six months you will find that meeting once per month is adequate. If your company or plant is large enough to support a Quality Performance Department (see **Figures 1-2 and 1-3**), that group should still meet weekly. The Quality Performance Department will manage the activities listed in the chapters to follow.

## MISSION STATEMENT

You will need to develop a Mission Statement. This provides focus for all activities that imply you will change the culture of your company from one traditionally ruled by manufacturing targets to one more sensitive to the needs of the customer. The

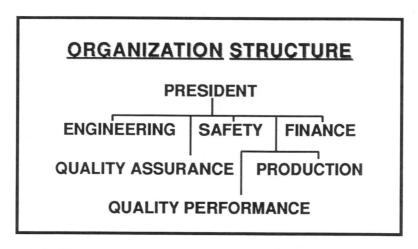

**FIGURE 1-2 : QUALITY PERFORMANCE DEPARTMENT WITH RESPECT TO THE ORGANIZATION**

**FIGURE 1-3 : THE QUALITY PERFORMANCE DEPARTMENT IS A SUB-COMMITTEE OF THE QUALITY STEERING COMMITTEE**

targets may require great improvements in quality. Quality should be thought of in terms of *vision, strategy,* and *culture,* not just *processes, techniques,* and *measures.* It should be a vision of achievement with some feel or direction to communicate it to everyone. A company can consider itself truly committed to quality only if every single employee is a participant and a believer.

A Mission Statement is not easy to produce. It may take several months to develop. You want to state what you intend to accomplish and how you will go about doing it. In writing, it might be best to define *product* as outputs by anyone in the system, *customer* as anyone who receives that output, and *everyone* as employees, suppliers, and those in the distribution and service systems. An example is shown in **Figure 1-4**.

## XYZ COMPANY MISSION STATEMENT

*We at XYZ Company are determined to make a product worthy of our customer's satisfaction.*

*Not only will our customers enjoy our product, they will recommend it to others.*

*Everyone of us can make an important contribution to attain this goal.*

*As we do our work, we will look for and eliminate waste and continuously try to improve our work.*

**FIGURE 1-4 : COMPANY MISSION STATEMENT**

## THE CHANGE

Quality starts with really understanding what customers require and how your competitors are trying to give it to them.  Remember, *quality* relates to your *profitability* (see **Figure 1-5**)

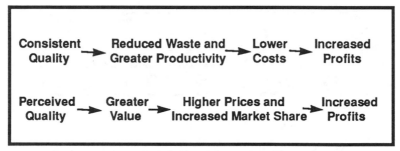

**FIGURE 1-5 : THE QUALITY / PROFITABILITY EQUATION**

Performance improvements involve the refinement of all physical and managerial processes. Improvement must be continual and people are the only source of ideas for improvement.  Most significant improvements require participation and buy-in by more than one department.  Every department is a Quality Department:  Quality Production;  Quality Accounting;  Quality Engineering; Quality Maintenance;  in addition to Quality Assurance.  Everyone owns quality, not just one group in the organization.  This may require an entire change in the company culture.  See how far along your company is with the New Participative Management Style (**Figure 1-6**).

## CULTURAL CHANGES TO OVERCOME

| *OLD STYLE* | *NEW STYLE* |
|---|---|
| - Delegated quality | - Lead by top management |
| - Quality as a tactic | - Quality as a fundamental business strategy |
| - Good enough | - Continuous improvement |
| - Quality as a feature | - Quality as a value |
| - Quantity | - Quality |
| - What is good for me? | - What is good for the customer? |
| - This is what we can give you | - What do you want? |
| - The Quality Department | - The Quality Company |
| - Maverick | - Teamwork |
| - Company secrets | - Partnerships with customers |
| - Looking good | - Being good |

FIGURE 1-6 : THE NEW PARTICIPATIVE
MANAGEMENT STYLE

# 22 QUALITY PERFORMANCE

To create the New Management System:

1. Educate people.

2. Lead the people at all levels of the organization

3. Identify and quantify the waste at all levels.

4. Enable everyone to work in this new system by changing the organization behavior (rules, policies, procedures).

Start small in your approach to implement this cultural change. Identify key factors and key activities. Throughout this book you will read how to start, participate in, and accomplish **QUALITY PERFORMANCE**. *Like success, quality is a journey, not a destination.*

To lead into your Quality Performance program, start with an awareness campaign. Chapter 2 will give you ideas for a successful kick-off and awareness program.

# CHAPTER 2

## QUALITY AWARENESS

**S**ince you have employees with a variety of backgrounds and experience, before you can **expect** Quality Performance, you have to make everyone **aware** of quality. That includes quality of your products, quality of each individuals own work, and quality of services given to your customers. This is the driving force behind a **QUALITY AWARENESS PROGRAM**. You want everyone to know that *"Quality starts with me"*.

---

# QUALITY - just what the Customer ordered.

## THE KICKOFF

You want to get everyone on the team working towards quality performance.  A splashy kickoff is a good way to get everyone's attention.  This can include various mechanisms:

- A banner announcing the new undertaking, displayed in a prominent location.

- Hang framed posters throughout the work place which depict various objects and slogans related to quality.  Many companies who sell these posters send them on a weekly or monthly basis so you can change them for a fresh look.

One company that sells these posters is:

Vantage Communications
Box 546
Hyack, NY  10960
Phone:  914-358-0147

- Have buttons made up with your company

# QUALITY is our signature.

logo and a quality slogan on it. Have buttons freely passed out to all employees encouraging to wear them everyday (for awhile). Set an example by making the Quality Steering Committee wear their buttons daily. Have plenty of extra buttons for anyone who lost his/her button, left it at home on another shirt, or wants extra buttons to take home for family and friends. Give these out freely to suppliers, customers, truck drivers, and anyone who stops by your business. You can easily spread the word of Quality Awareness.

Slogan examples are listed in blocks throughout this chapter. By adding your company logo, you can personalize any for your own use. You may want to create your own slogans. Later in this chapter are details on running your own Quality Slogan Contest.

- Have stickers made up with your company logo and quality slogans or themes. Use

> # QUALITY Products by QUALITY People.

these stickers freely on company/plant/office correspondence.

## ON-GOING

Once established, you will want to keep Quality Awareness in the forefront.  Here are a few ideas to accomplish this:

- Freely inform employees of any happenings with customers, suppliers, or related issues by use of bulletin board notices, as a regular feature in your company newspaper, or memos to every employee.

- Use bright paper for bulletin board announcements on Quality Performance issues.  Have a trademark of a certain symbol or letter to distinguish a note as one pertaining to Quality Performance.  An example might be using the letter "Q" on all the Quality Performance correspondence.

Some stationery outlets sell special theme paper at reasonable rates.  Here are three

---

# QUALITY is not an ACCIDENT.

suppliers of illustrated paper:

COPI-EZE Inc.
P.O. Box 64785
St. Paul, MN 55164
Phone: 1-800-843-0414
In MN: 612-636-3602

Idea Art
P.O. Box 291505
Nashville, TN 37229-1505
Phone: 1-800-433-2278

Memindex, Inc.
149 Carter Street, Box 139
Rochester, NY 14601
Phone: 716-342-7740

To minimize costs, purchase the minimum (approximately 25 sheets for $3 to $5 at a minimum order of $15 to $25). Use the color originals for the posted memos. Make

# TEAM QUALITY
# is the drive toward
# a perfect score.

copies in black and white for any additional sharing of information. Or you can buy larger quantities of the decorative paper at reduced volume rates.

- Have giveaways to mark special occasions (production record month, perfect attendance, best sales month, success obtaining a new customer, safety records achieved).

These giveaways can be theme related. Examples:

1. Wooden or mechanical pencils with a slogan and company logo to promote jotting down your good idea.

2. A key chain with the event inscribed on it for everyone.

3. A money clip with the company logo and the theme indicating increased sales or profits.

---

# QUALITY - YOU can make the difference.

- Use special note pads made with the quality slogans on the top or bottom for internal memos.

- Have calenders make with quality messages or slogans.  These can be the pop-up type or the page-per-month type.  Local vendors can supply you with samples.

## QUALITY SLOGAN CONTEST

To help promote Quality Awareness throughout your work place you need slogans.  As mentioned in this chapter, quality slogans can be used on stickers, buttons, stationery, promotion items, bulletin board notices, posters, and bumper stickers.  You can generate employee participation by having a Quality Slogan Contest.  Everyone can have fun coming up with wild and creative ideas and you will have plenty of slogans to use.

## TO RUN THE SLOGAN CONTEST:

1. Determine the judges before you start the contest.

---

# QUALITY makes CENTS.

It can be the Quality Steering Committee, the Quality Performance Department, or a predetermined selection of your choice.

2. Define the rules. Is artwork included in the contest? How will duplicates be handled (first one counts)?

3. Determine how long the contest will run. Two weeks to one month will allow people to think of ideas or create artwork.

4. Determine what the prizes will be and how many winners you will have. This is a good opportunity to have several first place winners. Each winner can get something with his/her slogan on it: a bumper sticker; a sign; a plaque. You may want to give out a company promotion item with the slogan on it to tie it into the company.

5. Make up colorful pre-printed forms and spread them generously throughout the work place. See **FIGURE 2-1** for an example.

---

# QUALITY is not a LUXURY, it is a NECESSITY.

---

# QUALITY SLOGAN CONTEST

**DATE :** _____

**TO :** Designated Receiver

**FROM :** _____

**MY QUALITY SLOGAN IS :**

**Q**

**DEADLINE :** (Date contest ends)

**FIGURE 2-1 :  QUALITY SLOGAN CONTEST ENTRY FORM**

6. Prepare and post bulletin board notices about the contest. Give all the pertinent information including who they can call if there are any questions.

7. The person receiving the slogans should prepare them for the judging. This could be as simple as covering the employee name when copying, or have them typed so the handwriting is not detectable.

8. After the contest deadline, pass out the anonymous copies of the slogans to the judges. The judging process can be either independent where each judge privately selects choices and gives them to the designated receiver. Or, it can be a group process where you hold a meeting and vote openly.

9. Determine the winners.

10. Notify the winners. Award the prizes. Put a notice on the bulletin board and take a picture of

---

# QUALITY is our
# ASSURANCE of
# satisfied CUSTOMERS.

each winner for your company paper.

11. Make use of the many slogans, *especially the winning ones*.

## QUALITY AWARENESS VIDEO

As you implement phases of the program, make sure you take plenty of photos and videos where ever possible. This is your success story. Many items to include are detailed throughout the book. Here is a summary list:

- An introduction from the President , Plant or Store Manager stating support of the Program.

- A Quality Steering Committee meeting in progress, introducing each member.

- The Quality Slogan Winners.

- The Quality Suggestion process through to winning (someone writing the idea, the

> # Our road to SUCCESS is paved with QUALITY.

Facilitator receiving it, the judging process, and announcing the winner).

- Quality suggestions implemented.

- A customer visit.

- Awards received from customers.

- A statistical / problem solving training session in progress.

- Statistical process control being utilized.

- A task team in action.

- A team presentation to the Quality Steering Committee.

- A team celebration.

- Any celebrations or special events.

- Your company Quality Policy on display.

# Today's QUALITY is tomorrow's SUCCESS.

- Statistical quality control charts sent to customers.

- Quality posters on display.

This is mentioned early in the book so you do not overlook or forget to take a permanent record of your success events. The collage can be organized on a story board (see **Figure 2-2**). By using this form you may find scenes you will want to add to your journal.

This video can be shown to all the employees (with cookies, fruit, and beverages) to make them aware of everyone's efforts. It can be sent to customers and suppliers to show how committed your organization is to **QUALITY**. Other locations within your organization can share progress and ideas by viewing each other's video. If video equipment is too expensive for your budget, add story lines to photographs and organize them in an album as a story of your program success.

However you choose to record your program is up to you, but remember to *do it*! It is much easier to

---

# QUALITY - the extra step to SUCCESS.

put a summary together after collecting the photos or video segments then having to start from scratch. Update on an as needed basis. And as you see the successes snowball, you will be wanting to toot your horn with everyone.

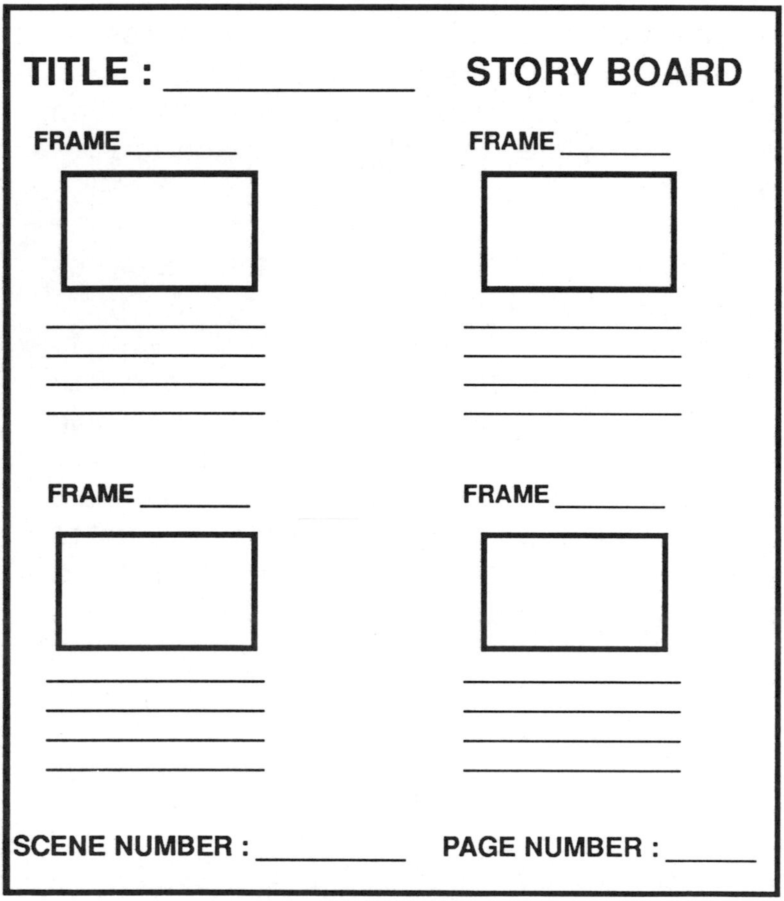

TITLE : _____    STORY BOARD

FRAME _____

FRAME _____

FRAME _____

FRAME _____

SCENE NUMBER : _____    PAGE NUMBER : _____

**FIGURE 2-2 : STORY BOARD FORM FOR ORGANIZING SCENES OR IDEAS**

# CHAPTER 3

## QUALITY SUGGESTION
## PROGRAM

**N**obody listens to me. How many times have you heard this from employees? One way to obtain employee participation it to establish programs based on the concerns and issues they identify. If the focus is on the individual or group interests and problems, motivation to participate will be easily generated. In addition to the slogans, buttons, posters, and other publicity items, you need a tool to enable all employees to share their ideas and suggestions for quality improvement. This can encompass the areas of your products, customer service, packaging, shipping, job performance, community image, and communication. The market place is increasingly competitive and you want to stress that *you* want to *win* the battle of having products and services better and lower priced while maintaining your reputation for quality. This is the purpose for having a **QUALITY SUGGESTION PROGRAM**, to let everyone get involved by participating in it.

## TO START - THE GROUNDWORK

It is ***most important*** to have management support for this program.  Support includes:

- visibility
- spoken commitment
- actions
- monetary backup

The Quality Steering Committee (or Quality Performance Department) needs to support it and ***enthusiastically*** promote it.  They need to be responsible for its fruition to be a successful program. Ideally, the Facilitators could be responsible for the legwork of the program.

As with the slogan contest, have one person designated to receive the Quality Suggestions.  This could be the Chief Facilitator.  As participants have questions, they could direct them to one person who may be able to answer them or able to get a quick response.

## CONTEST DETAILS

List the guidelines for the contest.  You will

probably want to prepare these with the Quality Steering Committee.  Items to consider:

1. Who is eligible to submit suggestions? Only employees, or are outsiders (visitors, friends, suppliers, customers, temporary help) permitted to participate too?

2. Determine the prizes.  Experience has shown not to give too much in the way of monetary rewards.  The goal is to improve quality, thus improve the longevity and profit picture of the company.  When employees want a percentage of the cost savings, you create new problems:

   - Someone must keep accurate track of the savings and the time period that the savings will be calculated.

   - How do you handle implemented suggestions that result in a loss to the company?

   - You begin setting an atmosphere of hostility amongst fellow employees if someone is not included in the suggestion, or did not submit the idea first.

   - Teamwork may deteriorate if people are afraid their good ideas will get stolen.

Keep the cash prizes in the range of:

**First** Prize : $50 to $100
**Second** Prize : $25 to $50
**Third** Prize : $10 to $25

3. Determine who is eligible for the cash prizes. It might be discouraging if the President, Plant / Store Manager, or one of the Staff wins the money prizes. You may want to disqualify them from receiving the money but not the recognition. If a manager wins, have them tie with the second place (or next place) winner and give the non-manager the cash prize. By this method, it will be clear to the other employees that the managers will not take the money or *"rig"* the contest. It will also enable managers to still receive recognition of their good, winning suggestions.

4. Make sure all the employees are notified about the Quality Suggestion Program. In addition to a bulletin board notice, give each employee a memo describing the contest, the rules, prizes, and a few example suggestions. Include with the memo several blank suggestion forms. **Figure 3-1** shows a sample form. Have copious amounts of blank forms placed in work areas, break rooms, secretary stations, and with each Facilitator. Make

# QUALITY SUGGESTION PROGRAM

**DATE :** _____

**TO :** Designated Receiver

**FROM :** _____

## My Quality Suggestion of :

- Job Performance
- Products
- Customer Service
- Packaging
- Office Procedures

- Maintenance
- Environment
- Utilities
- Plant Services
- Communication

- Housekeeping
- Shipping
- Office Services
- Community Image
- Waste Disposal

**IS :**

_____
_____
_____
_____
_____
_____
_____
_____
_____
_____

**Q**

**FIGURE 3-1 :  A BLANK QUALITY SUGGESTION FORM**

sure someone is responsible for receiving the suggestions. This gives employees a name they can contact if they have a question rather than just a department. Change the color of the form for each contest to help stimulate interest.

5. Plan to index the Quality Suggestions as they arrive. Dates on the suggestions will help determine which contest it qualifies in (by month, mid-month to mid-month, or the 28th of each month as the deadline). Some indexing suggestions:

> Month - Year - Suggestion Number
> 9-91-1
> 9-91-2
> 9-91-3

> Year - Contest - Suggestion Number
> 91-9-1
> 91-9-2
> 91-9-3

By using index numbers, the typed suggestions can be kept anonymous. Let only the Facilitators and the typist know who submits the suggestions on a regular basis. This will allow employees the freedom to make suggestions without the possibility of being ridiculed by fellow employees. Of course there will be times when suggestions will be identified:

- Winning suggestions should be posted on the bulletin boards with the suggestor's name.

- If a suggestion needs clarified, someone other than the Facilitators may need to speak to the suggestor.

- If a Task Team is formed, it is a good idea to include the suggestor on the team.

6. Set up an identification system on a personal computer (computer spreadsheets are ideal for this). It will correspond with your indexing system (**Figure 3-2**). This will enable easy referencing as data can be sorted:

- by name

- location (what area is most suggested)

- manager responsibility (who is getting a big load)

- suggestion outcome code (how many were rejected)

# QUALITY SUGGESTION INDEXING SYSTEM

| Suggestion Number | Contest Number | Suggestor | Brief Description | Area for Improvement | Outcome Code | Sent To | Status Update |
|---|---|---|---|---|---|---|---|
| 1 | Sept91 | Smith, Bob | Extend storeroom hours to 7AM-5PM | Storeroom | 4 | Storeroom Manager | |
| 2 | Sept91 | Jones, Mary | Get a microwave oven for lunchroom | Lunchroom | 3 - too expensive | | |
| 3 | Sept91 | Carry, Lynn | Give all office ee's a phone directory | Office | 1 | Office Manager | Done |

**FIGURE 3-2 : QUALITY SUGGESTION INDEXING SYSTEM**

7. Have a program to keep track of how many suggestions each employee submits per contest. This will help in selecting contest judges. You can see who did not submit a Quality Suggestion in that contest. You can also keep track of how many suggestions you received, who has not participated in the program, who submitted the most suggestions, and a breakdown of participation by area or department. **Figure 3-3** is an example setup.

8. Set the program to give everyone who submits a non-duplicate suggestion a token

# QUALITY SUGGESTION
# TRACKING LIST

| Name | | CONTEST | | | | | Running |
|------|-------|-------|-------|-------|-------|-------|-------|
| | Jun91 | Jul91 | Aug91 | Sep91 | Oct91 | Nov91 | Total |
| Adams, Joe | 1 | 5 | - | 1 | | | 7 |
| Billings, Pam | 2 | 1 | 1 | 1 | | | 5 |
| Brown, Mike | - | - | 1 | - | | | 1 |
| Carry, Lynn | - | 2 | 1 | 1 | | | 4 |
| Williams, Bill | 12 | 7 | 8 | 4 | | | 31 |
| Zest, Anna | - | 1 | 1 | - | | | 2 |

## FIGURE 3-3 :  TRACKING QUALITY
## SUGGESTIONS

for participating.  This can range from a sticker (costing pennies) up to a promotion item ($2 to $4 per item).  It is dependent upon what your budget can withstand.

Color coded stickers will help to advertise the program.  First place winner can receive a special gold sticker.  Have all other suggestors receive a silver sticker (see **Figure 3-4**).  Promote the idea of placing earned stickers on hardhats (if worn), lockers, plaques, or some other visible item.  This is something that the managers can receive as recognition if any win (tie) a suggestion contest.

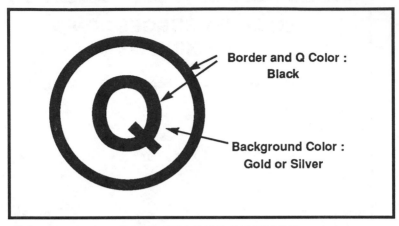

**FIGURE 3-4 : QUALITY SUGGESTION PROMOTION "Q" STICKER EXAMPLE**

Interest will really be stimulated if employees can obtain a promotion item for every suggestion submitted. Inexpensive items, bearing the company name and logo are wonderful in advertising the company and the suggestion program. To keep the interest generated, add a variety of promotion items to select from. National outlets can engrave or stencil your company name on pens, pencils, coffee mugs, tankards, shoe laces, note pads, rulers, hats, golf balls, thermometers, tote bags, tennis balls, socks, license plates, pocket knives, scarves, playing cards, key rings, - anything! Some nationally known outlets:

Best Impressions
348 North 30th Road
Box 800
LaSalle, IL 61301
Phone: 1-800-635-2378

Crestline Company, Inc.
22 West 21st Street
New York, NY 10010
Phone: 1-800-221-7797

Nelson Marketing, Inc.
210 Commerce Street
Oshkosh, WI 54901-0320
Phone: 1-800-722-5203
Fax: 414-236-7282

Rayod House, Inc.
P.O. Box 520 - QP
No. Arlington, NJ 07032

Have these items on hand when you start your program. When you give feedback to each suggestor, you can give each a sticker, another blank suggestion form, and ask what promotion item is wanted. It is exciting to see "Q" stickers on employees hard hats, lunch pails, lockers, or plaques at their work stations.

9. Composite the suggestions for each contest using the code system you chose

and distribute to the judges.  As mentioned, judges should be selected from employees who have not submitted a suggestion for that particular campaign.  If you have a mix of salary and hourly employees, try to have the same amount of judges from each group (example:  3 hourly and 3 salary judges).  Change the judges for each contest.  To assist the judges in their assignment, give them a packet of judging advice.  It could be similar to the following draft.

## QUALITY SUGGESTION JUDGING TIPS

a. Remember to judge the quality of the suggestions rather than the quantity of words in its write-up.  A one-liner could be as good or better than a whole page of a detailed suggestion.

b. Suggestions may be in different categories, but must be value-judged competitively for overall effect.  Think of what the suggestion you are evaluating would mean to someone's job, product, piece of equipment, or your customer.

c. Go through the whole list once, and make + or - or other symbols convenient to you, to distinguish good suggestions from those of lesser value.  That might cut your own working list in half.

d. Go through your +'d suggestions again and add a second + or some other symbol to the really superior ones to distinguish them from those that are just good. You may have 15 superior suggestions now to get into hard judging.

e. If necessary, repeat the + procedure to pare the list to exactly 10 before you start your numerical ranking procedure.

f. If there is not a lot of duplication among the judges lists, it may be necessary to meet with the Chief Facilitator to resolve the winners.

g. When ranking your top 10 lists, do not leave any ties between two or more suggestions. Take the time to distinguish the difference in fine points between them.

h. Send your top 10 lists back to the Chief Facilitator within one week. That would be by "month/day/year".

i. In deciding the winners, the Chief Facilitator will give your number 1 suggestion 10 points, your number 2 suggestion 9 points, down to your number 10 suggestion 1 point.  If a tie, those tied will split the prize money.

NOTE :  Do not forget to *thank the judges* with a memo for their efforts (**Figure 3-5**).

---

## XYZ COMPANY

MEMO
October 10, 1991

TO :  Bill Jones
     Marie Knappy
     Amy Lodge
     John Marks
     Mike Stevens
     Matt Young

FROM : The Chief Facilitator

Thank you for judging the September 1991 Quality Suggestion Contest.  Your efforts are appreciated. The winners will be notified in a few days

c :  Appropriate Supervisors

---

**FIGURE 3-5 :  THANK YOU NOTE TO THE QUALITY SUGGESTION CONTEST JUDGES**

10. Tally the judges scores to determine the winners. As listed in the Judging Advice, use a point system giving the best suggestion 10 points (in the top 10 lists), down to the 10th ranked suggestion 1 point. Add the scores per suggestion, the highest scoring suggestions are the winners (first, second, and third place winners).

11. Publicize the winners to add interest into the suggestion contest. Post a bulletin board notice. Take pictures of the winners receiving their prizes, for publication in your company newspaper. Employees like to see their name in print.

12. The Quality Performance Department should distribute the quality suggestions to the appropriate department, task team list, or back to the suggestor if not feasible or practical. The Quality Performance Department can review the suggestions giving each a code to simplify the process.

**QUALITY SUGGESTION DESTINATION CODE SYSTEM**

1 = Seems worth doing and a single department or person can easily accomplish. These suggestions are sent to the appropriate department head.

**2** = Seems worth doing but will require a task team to accomplish. Or, a task team is established and this suggestion pertains to the team goal topic.

**3** = Not worth doing either because it is not practical or too costly.

**4** = More information is needed to categorize this suggestion into the above codes **1**, **2**, or **3**.

Each suggestor should be advised of the status of her/his suggestion.

13. As suggestions are implemented, publicize them to show commitment of the company and help promote the contest.

14. Another way to spark interest in a suggestion contest is to have theme contests. Give an extra cash prize to the best suggestion falling in a special category. Here are two examples:

## CUSTOMER SERVICE CONTEST

Suggestions focusing on your customer:

- Services to customers

- Attractiveness of your packaging

- Accuracy of your weights

- Customer visits

- Improvements in transmitting information to customers, your warehouses, or your sales offices

- Timeliness of shipments

- Product promotions

- Truckdriver pick-ups at your location

- Publicizing your company, plant, store, or office

## COMMUNICATIONS CONTEST

Suggestions dealing with improvements of written, verbal, or visual communications:

- Between departments

- Between shifts

- With other locations

- With customers

- With suppliers

- With truckdrivers

- With fellow workers

- With supervisors

Other special categories you may want to consider:

- Safety
- Housekeeping
- Environment
- Time Management
- Packaging

You may want to have the Quality Performance Department judge the special contest. Allow the same suggestions to also be judged in the typical fashion to enable those eligibility for both contests (special and regular suggestion contest).

15. As packets of suggestions are prepared for judging, keep a packet to copy for circulation among the employees. Add a title page, such as the contest and number of suggestions (see **Figure 3-6**). Then make several copies of this packet. Place them in break rooms, locker rooms, lounge areas and the company library. You will be

XYZ COMPANY

# QUALITY SUGGESTION PROGRAM

## SEPTEMBER 1991
## CONTEST

# TOTAL SUGGESTIONS :

# 155 Q

FIGURE 3-6 : QUALITY SUGGESTION PACKET COVER PAGE

amazed at the interest everyone has in reading all the suggestions. These suggestions are always kept anonymous. This is not only a good advertising tool for the suggestion program, it also stimulates suggestions by many who read the packets.

A **QUALITY SUGGESTION PROGRAM** is beneficial in several ways. It promotes participation from employees; you have a tool to receive many good ideas; and you are able to recognize employees for their efforts. And *recognition* is one of the best rewards for good work!

# CHAPTER 4

## SPC IMPLEMENTATION

You may ask what is SPC and why do I want it? **SPC** is short for ***Statistical Process Control***. It works well in conjunction with teamwork and problem solving tools. Statistical charting alone does not solve problems or improve processes. Used with other tools, SPC is a valuable instrument. You cannot afford to sort, test, or inspect to get a Quality product or service. All your employees need to be trained in these tools.

In this chapter, topics to be discussed include the training and implementation of statistical charting of variables data and problem solving tools. Teamwork will be thoroughly discussed in the next two chapters.

Statistics, education and motivation take the

mystery out of Quality and make it attainable and measurable. Statistics allow you to have decisions based on **FACTS**, not **FEELINGS**. At a glance, one can see how consistent a process is with a Control Chart. Proper training will permit everyone to speak the same Quality Language. It is important to train *everyone*, not just the supervisors or professional staff.

People become interested in owning a responsibility when it benefits them. Benefits to be realized will be:

- reduced downtime
- reduced scrap or rework
- a better preventative maintenance schedule
- easier start-ups
- smooth operating conditions
- early warnings of a process change
- identifiable causes to problems
- easier shut downs

The bottom line to staying in business is meeting the Customer's expectations *every time*.

## TRAINING - MANAGERS, SUPERVISORS, PROFESSIONALS

Training can consist of two separate groups. Managers, supervisors, and professionals in one group and hourly and office services employees in another group. A distinction is made because supervisors and professionals need stronger training in statistics and problem solving methods to be able to grasp which tool to use or to interpret a chart. Further analysis may be required to determine critical variables, sources of variation, how processes vary, or what major changes need to be made which require capital expenses. They are the Leaders who will follow through and reinforce the new system.

An outside consultant or an in-house expert can explain statistical formulas and problem solving tools in more detail than would be necessary for the worker. A comprehensive training program for the hourly workers is in the next section of this chapter. However, this book will just list topics and procedures to include in your training sessions for the managers, supervisors, and professionals.

Training may require two to three days. Ideally, it will be off-sight so that interruptions will be at an absolute minimum. If you plan it during the work day, divide the group into at least two classes so not everyone is gone at the same time. If you are paying a consultant, consider holding the training on weekends. Allow attendees to compensate their time by scheduling off as their work schedules permit.

Items to review with the consultant or as you plan this training:

- Number of attendees per class

- Statistical and Problem Topics:

    1. Variation
    2. Flow Charts
    3. Brainstorming
    4. Pareto Charts
    5. Cause and Effect Charts
    6. Measurement
    7. Histograms
    8. Run Charts
    9. Control Charts
    10. Subgroups
    11. Teamwork
    12. Reward System

- Should attendees sit in small groups (teams)?

- Is assigned seating preferred?  This can allow a specific mix of employees by work areas, by strengths, or by job functions.

- Reserve the meeting location.

- Will there be evening training?  If yes, will dinner be provided?

- Will there be snacks (fruit, donuts, cheese & crackers, vegetables, beverages) during the breaks?

- Who will replenish the snacks?

- Is an overhead projector needed? If yes, make sure you have spare projector light bulbs.

- What training supplies are needed?

    - Pencils
    - Note Pads
    - Rulers
    - Flip Charts
    - Marking Pens
    - Projector Screen
    - Transparency Paper

- Will lunch be provided?

- Will statistical equipment be used?

    - Quincunx
    - Bead Box
    - Sampling Bowl

  **Note**: A supplier of these Statistical Instruments is:

    Quantum Company
    Box 431
    Clifton Park, NY 12065
    Phone: 518-877-5236

- Does everyone get a training manual?

- What is included in the manual?

- What should attendees bring?

    - Calculators
    - Pencil / Marker / Highlighter
    - Note Pad
    - Ruler

Invite every manager, supervisor and professional to this training. Personalized invitations are nice. An example invitation is shown in **Figure 4-1**. Careful planning will pay dividends in the form of smooth training, enthusiastic learners, minimized mishaps, and when treated as an ***important seminar***, attendees will carry that attitude back with them to their jobs.

At the end of the training session, give everyone an assignment pertaining to their work areas. The assignment would be something in the form of utilizing a new skill to help identify an existing problem. Some examples:

- Run charting a process variable like reaction temperature.

- Pareto charting customer complaints by product or profitability.

- Charting percentage of defects.

- Cause and effect diagram of office temperature fluctuations.

The Facilitator should follow-up on the assignments with each person.  Employees will get to see the benefits of these new tools by using them in their work. *Remember, use it or lose it!*

---

**John Monroe:**

**You are invited to attend our**
**Statistical Process Control**
**and**
**Problem Solving Training**
**2 - Day Seminar**

Date:  September 19 & 20, 1991
Time:  8:00 AM - 5:00 PM
Place:  Elegant Hotel, Our Town, USA

Bring:  Yourself and your imagination.
Snacks, manuals, pencils, markers,
calculators, rulers and lunch will
be provided.

Notify our Chief Facilitator if you cannot attend.

---

**FIGURE 4-1 :  PERSONALIZED INVITATION FOR THE TRAINING CLASS**

At the end of the training session, have a short graduation ceremony.  Give each attendee a certificate of course completion (see **Figure 4-2**) personalized in calligraphy.  Have the President or Plant Manager sign each one.  Call each person up by name to give him or her the certificate.  Finish by taking a group photo.  Give everyone a copy of the photo to remember the course training.

---

# XYZ COMPANY LOGO

## Quality Performance Training

### (Employee's Full Name)

has completed the Quality Performance seminar in

## Statistical Process control
## and
## Problem Solving

_____
**President / Plant Manager**

_____
**Course Facilitator**

_____
**Date**

---

**FIGURE 4-2 :  TRAINING CERTIFICATE**

**Note**: Calligraphy adds a tailored look to certificates, invitations, documents or any other papers. You can mail your materials to be written in calligraphy to:

> Eileen M. Stephenson
> Calligrapher
> 809 N. Grandview Avenue
> McKeesport, PA 15132

# TRAINING - HOURLY AND OFFICE SERVICES EMPLOYEES

This training can be accomplished in-house if you have a meeting room facility. Your Facilitators should be able to train small groups in one-day sessions. Benefits of having Facilitators conduct the training include:

- employees know the Facilitators

- class examples can be tailored for each class

- classes can be scheduled with a short lead time

- supervisors can sit in at no extra charge

- if employees have questions after the training, they can freely ask a Facilitator at any time

Items to consider in planning your training sessions:

- How many attendees per class?  Training groups are ideal between 8 to 16 people for each session.  This provides close interaction with everybody and allows people some freedom to express their ideas and opinions.

- Topics to teach (see the Training Manual Section in this chapter).

- Meeting room availability and number of tables and seats available.

- How many Facilitators should teach per session.  More than one is advised.  A full day of talking and teaching is difficult for one person.  Having at least two Facilitators also allows for more attention to details to each attendee.

- If you have two Facilitators training at each session, they can alternate between topics.

- Will you supply lunch?  It is a nice gesture if you do?  Buffet style of sandwiches and salad is healthy and light.  Invite managers to lunch with the group.  They can socialize with the employees.

- Coffee, juice, donuts, and fruit are good to have at the start of class. If the attendees did not eat breakfast, they can take advantage of the snacks.

- A 3-ring binder style Training Manual is easy to put together. Pages can be easily added or subtracted to enable you to tailor the training of each class. Attendees will feel special and be able to follow the examples from their work areas. Training Manuals can easily be made by copying a master on your copy machine onto 3-hole paper.

- Can you afford inexpensive calculators ($5 range) to give to everyone? If not, specify that they each bring one to class or have enough available to use during the class.

- Have plenty of pencils available. If you have pencils printed with a Quality Slogan, use them. Make sure a pencil sharpener is in the room. Have colored pencils or highlighter markers available too. The colored pencils or highlighters will be used on the charts for special points:

> - out-of-control
> - trends
> - clusters

- One color, such as red, is enough to identify

these type of points.

- Give everyone a ruler or straight edge.  This will be helpful when charting (center line and control limits).  As suggested with the pencils, have a Quality Slogan imprinted on the ruler or straight edge.

- Do you have adequate training supplies available?

  - Overhead Projector
  - Blank Overhead Transparencies
  - Overhead Marking Pens
    (erasable type)
  - Pointers
  - Flip Charts
  - Enough Flip Chart Pads
  - Masking Tape
  - Spare Calculators
  - Pencil Sharpener
  - Cardboard for Name Tents
  - A Statistical Tool

    - Quincunx
    - Bead Box
    - Sampling Bowl

- Can transparencies be made on your copy machine?  If not, you may consider taking the Training Manual to a place that can make transparency copies.  It is easy to follow along in class if you use transparencies for all or most pages of the workbook.

- Get cardboard or heavy paper for name tents. If you cannot have the tents preprinted before the class, have enough black marker pens on the tables so each person can write his / her name. It helps the trainers in calling everyone by first names during the session.

- Separate the tables to have employees sitting in small groups. This will start them working together in groups or teams - *teamwork*! Determine if you want assigned seating. If you do, make the name tents ahead of time. Before class place the tents where you want the people to sit.

- Determine how many breaks you shall have during the session. Be considerate of the attendees who have enjoyed the beverages, snacks and lunch. Allow enough time to let everyone use the rest rooms.

- As with training for the managers, supervisors, and professionals, have certificates made up to give each employee upon completion of the class (as shown in **Figure 4-2**). Personalize each, using calligraphy to add that extra touch of importance.

- Can your budget withstand a souvenir coffee mug or ball cap to give to each class graduate? Use a theme related to training. Two examples:

  **"I've been SPC'D"**
  **"I know my SPC's"**

- When scheduling the people to attend, try keeping them in natural work groups. This will help foster the concept of teamwork. Given the opportunity, people working together in their own environment can identify and solve many of the problems themselves, depending upon the complexity of the problem.

# TRAINING MANUAL (ONE-DAY SESSION)

This is a manual example for the training to be given to the *hourly and office services employees*. It keeps statistics simple, so as not to scare or confuse anyone with complex formulas. Allow plenty of space for each page so notes can be taken in the manual. Tools and examples for continuous improvement will be covered stressing the importance to do the job right the first time, relying on the workers to be responsible for their own work.

## CONTENTS

1. INTRODUCTION
Tell the class what you plan to cover in the course.

2. PROCESS MANAGEMENT
Define that a process is anything that does work.
Include flow charting, and customer and supplier
identification.

3. PROBLEM SOLVING
Brainstorming, Pareto charts, and cause and effect
charts are covered in this section.

4. STATISTICS
Statistics will include: normal process
characteristics, histograms, run charts, control
charts, control limits, and out-of-control signals.

5. VARIATION
Variation will be defined and demonstrated by use
of a Statistical tool (Quincunx, bead box, or sample
bowl) to run a *"production"* experiment.

6. X-MOVING RANGE CHARTS
Show an example of these type of charts. This is
a good time to make it an example of something in
the work area of the class.

7. PROCESS CAPABILITY
Process capability is defined. Demonstrate how
control limits relate to specification limits.

8. TEAMS
Define teamwork, how teams operate, and
member responsibilities.

9. APPENDIX
Have a glossary of terms, extra blank charts, and blank note paper.

# SECTION 1 : INTRODUCTION

Explain why you are meeting and having this training. *It is really to stay in business.* Quality means meeting the customer's expectations *every time*. You have to keep up with technology. Quality is now being connected with productivity, profitability, market share, safety, and environment. Tools that will be covered in the session:

1. Team problem solving tools

- Flow Chart
- Brainstorming
- Pareto Chart
- Cause and Effect Chart

2. Statistical Tools

- Histogram
- Run Chart
- Control Chart
- Control Limits
- Signals

3. Teamwork

Participation = Commitment

## SECTION 2 : PROCESS MANAGEMENT

A *process* is anything that does work. It has *inputs*, *outputs*, *suppliers*, and *customers* (**Figure 4-3**). Think of some example of internal and external suppliers and customers for the different groups you teach. Have them think of some examples during class. Here are two examples:

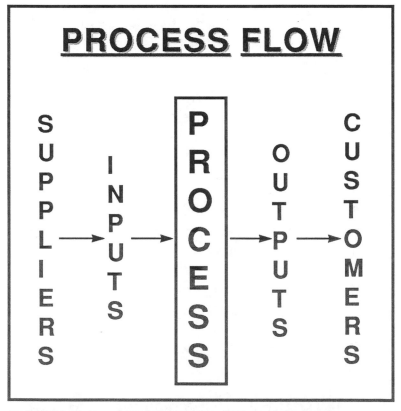

FIGURE 4-3 : PROCESS FLOW DIAGRAM

# 74 QUALITY PERFORMANCE

1. **PROCESS** = Quality Laboratory of a manufacturing company.

   **SUPPLIERS** = Each production unit, external raw material suppliers, glass companies for the glassware.

   **INPUTS** = Samples, paperwork, chemicals, glassware, request sheets.

   **OUTPUTS** = Sample results, paperwork, phone calls (to report the lab results), used samples.

   **CUSTOMERS** = Each production unit, company customers, the shipping department, the trash hauler.

2. **PROCESS** = Accounting Department

   **SUPPLIERS** = Employees with purchase requisitions, external companies owing you payment, computer company.

   **INPUTS** = Invoices, note pads, calculators, computer, computer software.

   **OUTPUTS** = Checks, paid invoices, information.

   **CUSTOMERS** = Employees, external suppliers receiving payments, the IRS.

A *process* is a combination of *materials*, *methods*, *people*, *environment*, *machinery*, and *measurement*. This could be as complex as a production unit or as simple as making coffee. When you define the process, you can see where changes can be made, where to collect data, and maybe where to eliminate steps. By controlling your processes, you will realize:

- better, more consistent quality
- better utilization of resources
- higher morale
- employees will be able to do a better job with less confusion
- less effort required to make a quality product
- economic benefits -- *Quality Sells!*
- waste costs money

# FLOW CHART

To easily see a process, draw a *flow chart* (**Figure 4-4**). A flow chart is a simple picture of how the process works. It includes all the steps in how the job gets done and it helps point out where there may be problems or something that could corrupt the process. A flow chart can:

- detect obvious redundancies and inefficiencies in the work flow.

- identify places for data collection and control chart work.

- allow everyone to have a common understanding of the process.

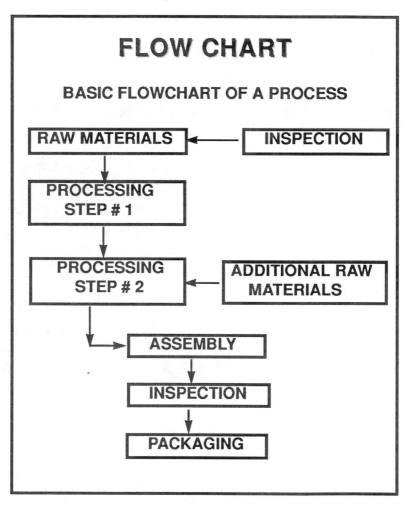

FIGURE 4-4 : BASIC FLOW CHART OF A PROCESS

# SECTION 3 : PROBLEM SOLVING

What would it be like if everything in your system was the **best** you could imagine it to be? There are no fires to put out and everything is in great shape. When you have done this, a goal has been **IMAGINEERED** for you to work towards achieving. How do you get there? This is the basis for **problem solving**.

- Access where you actually are relative to your imagineered goal.

- Challenge *every* detail of the operation. How? What? Where? Why? Who? When?

- Can you change or improve anything?

The following three tools will help to generate ideas (*brainstorming*), prioritize them (*Pareto chart*), and determine all possible causes (*cause and effect chart*).

## BRAINSTORMING

**Brainstorming** is a method to generate ideas. One person, usually a team/group Leader or Manager, will conduct the session. The generally accepted guidelines are:

- Never criticize ideas.

- Write on a flip chart or chalk board every idea. Having the ideas visible to everyone at the same time avoids misunderstandings and reminds others of new ideas.

- Make sure everyone understands the question or issue being brainstormed. Have it written down for everyone to see.

- Allow a few minutes for creative *"think time"* before starting.

- Generate a large number of ideas. Record the words of the speaker on the flip chart or chalk board. Do not interpret anything said.

- Encourage creative thinking.

- Everyone has an equal chance to participate.

- Do it quickly, 5 to 15 minutes work well.

- Participants should not interrupt each other.

Then:

- Make sure everyone understands each item on the list. Clarify any item as necessary.

- Eliminate the duplicates.

- Combine the similar items.

- Select the top ideas to work on by group vote.

Creative juices can really flow during this exercise. You will benefit by receiving tons of ideas, many which may be worth pursuing. And by giving everyone a chance to participate, no one will feel left out. When teaching, run a brainstorming session on something unrelated to work. Examples for topics:

- How to make more money.
- How to have a good marriage.
- How to get better gas mileage.
- Ecology ideas for the community.

## PARETO CHART

The **Pareto Chart** is also known as the *80/20 Rule* of the vital few versus the trivial many. A Pareto chart is a vertical bar graph illustrating problems in order of severity, frequency, or cost. It allows you to see the relative importance of all the problems or conditions in order to choose the starting point for problem solving, monitoring success or identifying the basic cause of a problem. **Figure 4-5** is an example of a Pareto chart. Some other examples:

- A few customers account for the majority of sales.

- A few products account for the majority of off-spec rejects.

- A few pieces of equipment account for the majority of down time.

- A few employees account for the majority of absenteeism.

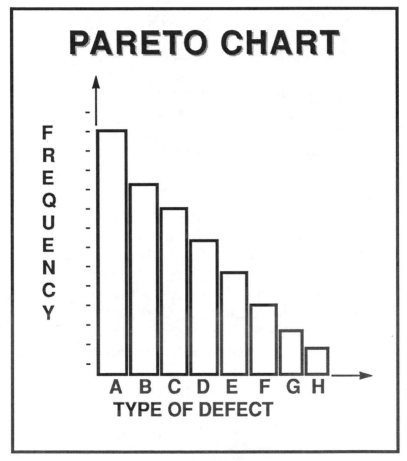

FIGURE 4-5 : A PARETO CHART
DEMONSTRATING FREQUENCY VERSUS TYPE
OF DEFECT

**Construction a Pareto Chart:**

1. Select the problems that are to be compared and ranked by order.

2. Select the standard for comparison unit of measurement (cost, frequency, easiest to fix, customer's biggest concern).

3. Select the time period to be studied (8 hours, one week, 20 weeks, one year).

4. Gather the necessary data for each category.

5. Compare the frequency or cost of each category relative to all other categories.

6. List the categories from left to right on the horizontal axis in order of decreasing frequency or cost. Categories containing the fewest items can be combined into an *"other"* category, which is placed on the extreme right as the last bar.

7. Above each classification or category, draw a rectangle of height representing the frequency or cost in that classification.

# CAUSE AND EFFECT CHART

**Cause and Effect Charts** are also called

*Fishbone Charts* because they look like a fish when constructed (**Figure 4-6**). The cause and effect chart was developed to represent the relationship between some *effect* and all the possible *causes* influencing

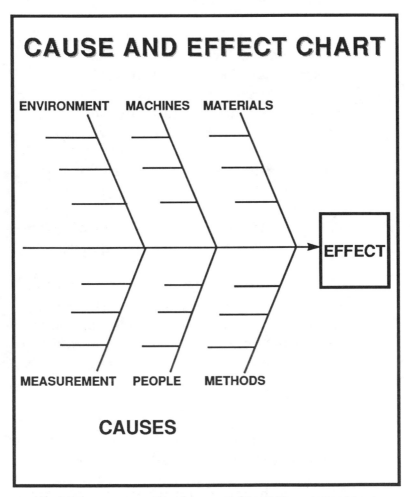

FIGURE 4-6 : A BLANK CAUSE AND EFFECT CHART

it.  For every effect there are likely to be several major categories of causes.  These causes might be summarized under the categories:

> Materials
> Methods
> People
> Environment
> Machinery
> Measurement

A well detailed cause and effect chart will take on the shape of fish bones.  Steps in constructing a cause and effect chart:

1. Agree on one statement that describes the problem(s).

2. Generate the causes needed to build the chart (via brainstorming).

3. Place the problem statement in the box on the right.

4. Draw the six major categories.

5. Place the brainstormed ideas in the appropriate major categories.

6. For each cause list what happens as it branches off the major causes.

7. Use as few words as possible.

8. Look for causes that appear repeatedly.

9. Reach consensus as a group.

10. Gather data to determine the relative frequencies of the different causes (Pareto chart).

The cause and effect chart:

- directs group thinking
- avoids jumping to a solution
- helps sort out causes
- shows relationship of causes

## SECTION 4 : STATISTICS

**Statistics** are used to further understand the process and determine whether it is consistent. Use of statistics help you to measure the degree of a known problem, spot potential problems, or to make sure a process remains problem free.

By using statistics, you will be able to identify normal process variation and excessive variation, decide when to take corrective action, and determine if implemented solutions are effective.

*Normal variation* in a process will result in a normal curve (bell-shaped curve, **Figure 4-7**). For this text, a normal curve will be defined as in control with 99.7% of the measured values falling between the bell curve of +3 and -3 standard deviations of the average.

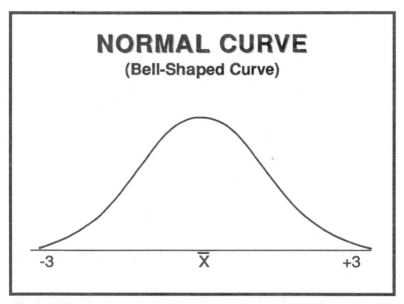

# NORMAL CURVE
### (Bell-Shaped Curve)

-3        $\overline{X}$        +3

FIGURE 4-7 : NORMAL BELL-SHAPED CURVE

## HISTOGRAM

A **histogram** takes measurement data (temperature, length, weight, time) and displays its distribution. A histogram reveals the amount of variation that any process has within it. A typical histogram would look like **Figure 4-8**.

The data in this figure is pictured normal in that ·the greatest number of units are at the center

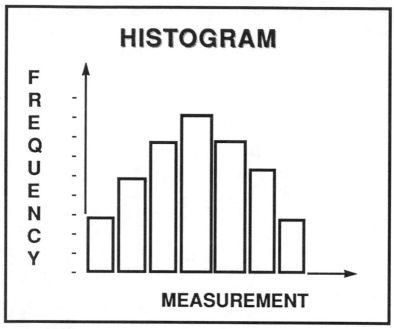

**FIGURE 4-8 : A HISTOGRAM SHOWING NORMAL DISTRIBUTION**

measurement with roughly an equal number of units falling on either side. Construction of a histogram will help show if your process is normal. or falling in the bell-shaped curve. It may show your data is skewed (slanted) to the left or right, or if the spread of data falls within specifications.

## RUN CHART

**Run Charts** are graphs of data points in time order (**Figure 4-9**). Data can be measurements, counts, or percentages of a product or characteristic.

Run Charts may illustrate trends, shifts in the average, or cycles. These are simple to use and easy to train. They are usually a preliminary step to using control charts.

Construction of a Run Chart:

- A marked point is the measurement observed at one point in time.

- Data points should be connected for easy use and interpretation.

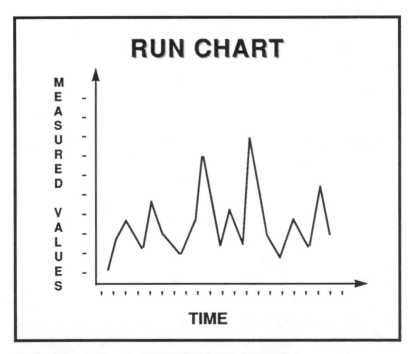

**FIGURE 4-9 : A RUN CHART GRAPH**

- Time period covered and unit of measurement must be clearly marked.

- Collected data must be kept in the order that it was gathered. Since it is tracking over time, the sequence of data points is critical.

## CONTROL CHART

**Control Charts** are similar to run charts but include additional data of control limits and the average over a given amount of data. **Figure 4-10** is an illustration of a control chart. Control limits define the amount of variation to be expected if the process is consistent over time. Control limits are calculated from actual process data. They are +3 and -3 standard deviations of the average.

Run your process, untouched, collecting data. At least 20 points will allow for accurate control limits to be calculated in the appropriate formula. You can now plot the points onto a chart to determine whether any of the points fall between the outside of the limits or form unnatural patterns. If either of these happen, the process is said to be *"out-of-control"*. The fluctuation of the points within the control limits is a result of the natural variation built into the process. Control limits and the center line can be related to precision and accuracy. **Precision** is the degree to which repeated measurement of the same unit result in the same value (control limits). **Accuracy** is the average of many repeated measurements of a certain unit equalling a *"correct"* value (center line).

Remember that even if a process is **in control** it does not necessarily mean that the product or service will meet your needs.  It only means that the

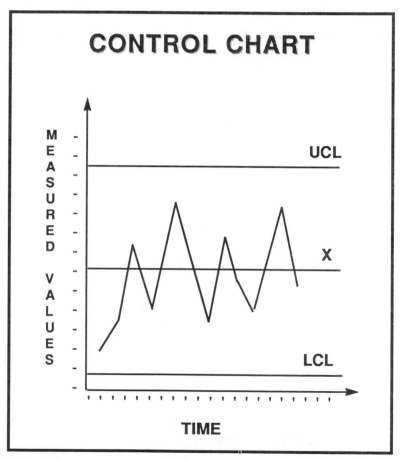

**FIGURE 4-10 : A CONTROL CHART GRAPH**

process is consistent.  If your process is in control but out of specifications, you need to either change your process or the specifications.  Management controls the natural variation between control limits.

A control chart is out-of-control if:

- one or more points fall outside the control limits

- nine successive points fall on one side of the center line

- seven consecutive points either are increasing or decreasing

- fourteen points in a row alternating up and down

Investigate an out-of-control process:

- Is the same measuring device being used?

- Are there accuracy differences in the measurement instruments, if more than one are used?

- Are there differences in the methods used by different operators?

- Is the process affected by the environment?

- Is the process affected by equipment wear?

- Has there been a change in the raw materials?

- Is the process affected by operator fatigue?

- Has maintenance been recently done on the equipment?

- Did the samples come from different machines? shifts? operators?

- Are operators afraid to report bad data?

Statistics can be related to everyone's life:

- The TV rating system as to which shows are renewed and which are canceled.

- TV commercials are different for various events:

    - Sporting events = trucks, alcohol
    - Soap operas = cleaning products, coffee, feminine hygiene products
    - Cartoons = toys, cereals, candy

- Auto insurance rates are based on statistics of age, location, number of drivers, number of vehicles, type of vehicle, national averages, number of incidents.

In summary, you will need to:

- gather statistics on the process or operation.

- develop and use charts.

- identify the special causes and common causes of problems by statistical means.

- fix the special causes, that is those not common to the process. A special cause is a source of variation not inherent in the process. It is intermittent, unpredictable, unstable, and usually assignable. A common cause is a source of variation that is always present. It is part of the random variation inherent in the process.

- have support from management to fix the common causes by changing the system.

## SECTION 5 : VARIATION

Unless your measuring device is not sensitive enough, you will see **variation** in anything measured. Nothing is exactly alike. Variation is the inevitable difference among individual outputs of a process. Control charts take this into account by use of the control limits. Expect variation. Management determines what is too much variation by the control limit signal. They decide where to spend money to make process changes.

A good statistical tool to demonstrate process variation is the **Quincunx Box (Figure 4-11)**. The

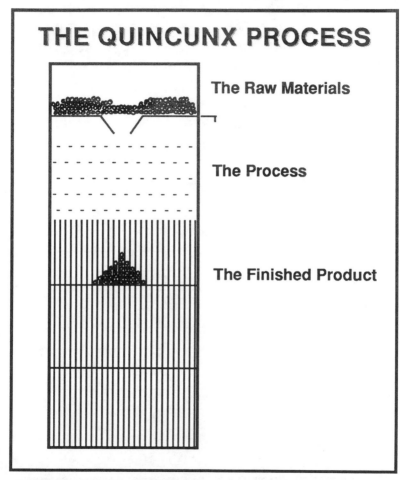

**THE QUINCUNX PROCESS**

The Raw Materials

The Process

The Finished Product

**FIGURE 4-11 : THE QUINCUNX STATISTICAL TOOL USED FOR VARIATION EXPERIMENTS**

*machine* is the box itself. The *material* is the beads before entering the slots. The *method* will be the dropping one bead at a time down into the slots. Pre-number the slots to identify them. The *measurement* will be the numbered slot the bead falls into. The *product* will be identified as the beads in the slots. The *people* will be the class members playing the roles of operators and inspectors. And the *environment* will be the classroom.

Fill in the chart in **Figure 4-12** with the production of beads. Use several people as *"shifts"*.

## QUINCUNX EXPERIMENT

| Subgroup | X | R | Subgroup | X | R |
|:---:|:---:|:---:|:---:|:---:|:---:|
| 1 | | | 11 | | |
| 2 | | | 12 | | |
| 3 | | | 13 | | |
| 4 | | | 14 | | |
| 5 | | | 15 | | |
| 6 | | | 16 | | |
| 7 | | | 17 | | |
| 8 | | | 18 | | |
| 9 | | | 19 | | |
| 10 | | | 20 | | |
| TOTAL : | | | TOTAL : | | |

FIGURE 4-12 : QUINCUNX EXPERIMENT LOG SHEET

Let groups (operator and inspector) make 5 to 10 beads each. It gets many involved. Have everyone plot the bead values on a histogram (**Figure 4-13**) so all will have a copy of the curve. Then plot the points on an X-Moving Range chart (**Figure 4-14**). Calculate the averages and control limits using the formulas in **Figure 4-15**.

Statistics alone will not cause improvement. They merely transmit information to the people.

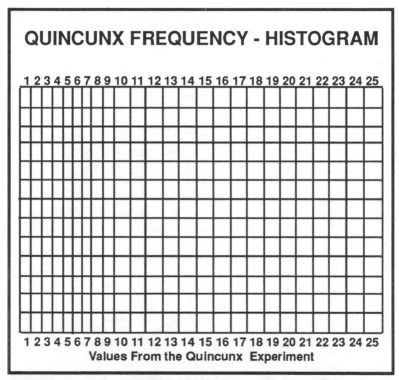

FIGURE 4-13 : HISTOGRAM FORM FOR THE QUINCUNX EXAMPLE

People (workers, teams, management) are the receivers of the transmissions and decide when and what to respond and change.

After the class example, look at the charts to see if they are consistent. Review the out-of-control conditions for control charts listed in Section 4. If any point(s) is out-of-control, is there an assignable cause? Have plenty of class discussion to understand how to read the charts.

This is a fun example that easily demonstrates

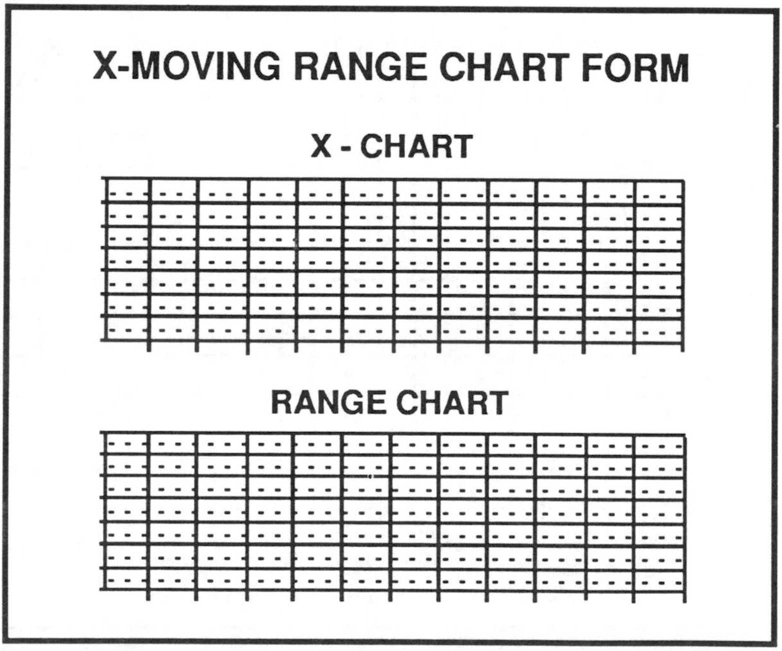

**X-MOVING RANGE CHART FORM**

**X - CHART**

**RANGE CHART**

**FIGURE 4-14 : X-MOVING RANGE CHART FORM**

process variation. You can also point out how variation is a natural occurrence such as people's height or the weather from day to day Ask for some other examples from the class to confirm understanding of variation.

---

## WORK SHEET FOR X AND R CHARTS

**FACTORS :   FOR   n = 2**

k   = No. of individual readings =   _____

$D_3$ = Factor for R chart (in Table) =   none

$D_4$ = Factor for R chart (in Table) =   3.27

$d_2$ = Factor for computing std. dev. (in Table) =   1.128

( Note :  Table of constants can be found in a statistical manual)

|  | R Chart | X Chart |
|---|---|---|
| Central Line | $\bar{R} = \dfrac{\text{Total of R Values}}{\text{No. of R Values}}$  $\bar{R} = \dfrac{R}{k-1} =$ | $\bar{X} = \dfrac{\text{Total of X Values}}{\text{No. of Samples}}$  $\bar{X} = \dfrac{X}{k} =$ |
| Upper Control Limit | $UCL_R = D_4 \times \bar{R}$  $UCL_R =$ | $UCL_X = \bar{X} + \dfrac{3\bar{R}}{d_2}$  $UCL_X =$ |
| Lower Control Limit | $LCL_R = D_3 \times \bar{R}$  $LCL_R =$ | $LCL_X = \bar{X} - \dfrac{3\bar{R}}{d_2}$  $LCL_X =$ |

**FIGURE 4-15 :  WORK SHEET FOR X AND R CHARTS, FORMULAS INCLUDED ON WORK SHEET**

# SECTION 6 : X-MOVING RANGE CHARTS

When you have a process where measurements are available on a limited schedule, or it is feasible to take data on intervals (hourly, twice a shift, or less frequently), you want to compare that with the control chart. For this reason, each point is plotted separately on an X-Moving Range Chart. Our Quincunx example is this type of chart. The subgroup size is one.

Run through another example of gathering data. Before the class, prepare an example from the class work area. This example will be best understood if it pertains to their actual process. Select one variable to collect data. Get the last 20 to 40 data points. Mark each value on a note card. Put them in a *"hat"* or bag to draw from. Have blank forms to fill out for everyone ( **Figures : 4-16, 4-13, 4-14, and 4-15**). Also chart the data in its actual time sequence to share with the class after the exercise. This part of the exercise will demonstrate the importance of *time entered data*.

Walk around the room letting everyone pick a value. Continue until the *"hat"* is empty. Then plot the histogram and X-Moving Range Chart, calculating the average and control limits. Now show the class what a difference time-ordering makes. The histograms will look the same but you should see some variation in the control limit calculations and the appearance of the data on the control chart.

## CLASS EXAMPLE : _____

| # | X | R | # | X | R | # | X | R |
|---|---|---|----|---|---|----|---|---|
| 1 | | | 11 | | | 21 | | |
| 2 | | | 12 | | | 22 | | |
| 3 | | | 13 | | | 23 | | |
| 4 | | | 14 | | | 24 | | |
| 5 | | | 15 | | | 25 | | |
| 6 | | | 16 | | | 26 | | |
| 7 | | | 17 | | | 27 | | |
| 8 | | | 18 | | | 28 | | |
| 9 | | | 19 | | | 29 | | |
| 10 | | | 20 | | | 30 | | |

**FIGURE 4-16 : BLANK DATA COLLECTION FORM FOR THE CLASS EXAMPLE**

# SECTION 7 : PROCESS CAPABILITY

Take the time to talk about standard deviation and show what it looks like on a normal distribution curve (**Figure 4-17**). **Standard Deviation** is a measure of the spread of the process output. It is interesting to see the difference of one, two, and three standard deviations. This will help set the tone to discuss process capability.

**Process Capability** refers to the ability of a process to produce units whose measurements will range over a band of values narrow enough so that

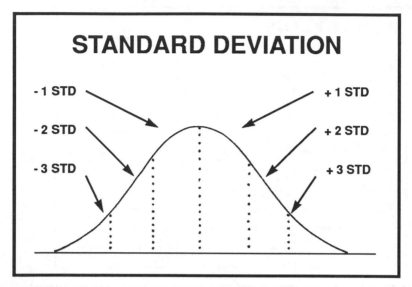

FIGURE 4-17 : ONE, TWO, AND THREE
STANDARD DEVIATIONS ON A NORMAL CURVE

proper centering of the process average will result in products falling within specification limits.

**PROCESS CAPABILITY =**

$$\frac{\text{Specification Range}}{\text{(Upper - Lower) Control Limits}}$$

If the Process Capability formula is *less than one*, the process is *not capable*. If it *equals or is greater than one*, your process *is capable*. It may require adjusting the process average to fit the control limits within the specification limits. **Figure 4-18** shows data curves with relation to specification limits. You can explain process capability pictorially.

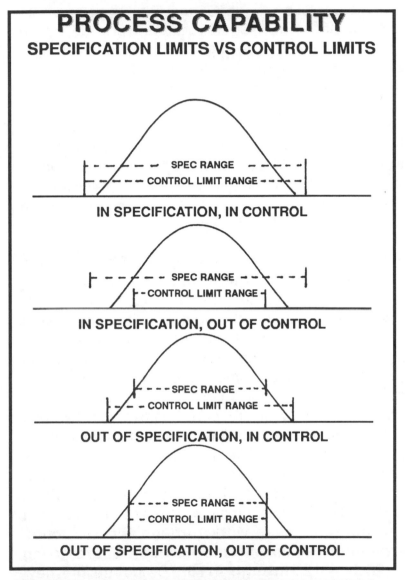

**FIGURE 4-18 : PROCESS CAPABILITY VERSUS SPECIFICATION LIMITS**

Now let's talk about the Quincunx example back in Section 5. Specifications were not talked about at that time. Looking at your curve, make up a specification range which will **easily** result in a process capability greater than one. With the class, walk through the calculation. From your example, you should have the upper and lower control limits. Now tell the class you have a new customer who wants a huge amount of red beads of specification "X to Y". Let "X to Y" be values which fall between the previous calculated control limits, thus would result in a process capability of less than one.

Ask the class what should be done if they were the team to solve this dilemma. Do you sort production for this customer? That means 100% inspection. Also, now the other customers will see a change in the material they receive. It will be mostly high and low values and not much in the middle. Do you tell the new customer tough luck, take what is given to them? Or do you try to change (improve) the process? The Quincunx board comes with two peg board sets. Use the peg board with more variation in the first example (Section 5). Tell the class management has agreed to your recommendation of improving the process. Then change the peg board to the one with less variation. Show the class both peg boards. Then work through the Quincunx experiment again with the new peg board, using **Figures 4-12 through 4-15.** Calculate the new control limits and see if your process capability for the new customer improves (*it should!*). This example will help demonstrate both process capability and process improvement.

# SECTION 8 :  TEAMS

A **Team** is a group of individuals who are committed to achieving common objectives; who work and interact openly and effectively together; and who produce high quality results.

**Benefits** of teamwork:

- Can get a better problem definition
- Several contributors
- Input from "experts"
- High quality decisions
- High involvement, motivation, and commitment
- Ownership of solutions
- Strength in numbers
- Win-Win solution

Team member **Responsibilities** include:

- Participate
- Help keep the meeting on track
- Help pick problems
- Collect data
- Analyze data
- Recommend solutions
- Implement solutions
- Evaluate solutions

More on *TEAMWORK* is detailed in the next chapter.

# SECTION 9 : APPENDIX

Have a glossary of terms, extra blank charts and some note paper in this section. Terms included in the examples are:

$n$ = Sample size or subgroup size
$k$ = Number of samples or subgroups
$X$ = Value or reading
$\overline{X}$ = Average value
$R$ = Subgroup range
$\overline{R}$ = Average range
$s$ = Standard deviation

# IMPLEMENTATION PLAN

Now that your training is complete you will want to implement Statistical Process Control in your work areas where you find it applicable. Members of the Natural Improvement Teams (Chapter 6), with Facilitator involvement as necessary, are the best to determine what needs charted. When you do decide that charting is practical and useful, begin with Run Charts. They are simple to use and will allow you to collect preliminary data for your Control Charts. Data from the Run Charts can be used to calculate control limits. Starting with run charts also helps employees get familiar with charting. As you phase into control charts, the Natural Team should review action plans for the control charts.  Charts will not be effective to the employee if they do not know what action steps to take when situations occur.  Items to review:

- Out-of-control points
- Trends
- Clusters of data
- Key charts
- What are the assignable causes?
- Should anyone be called under certain conditions?
- What are the key variables?

## RAW MATERIALS

If you check quality variables of incoming raw materials, or accept on the basis of a Certificate of Analysis, you should plot the results.  Employees should be aware of normal from abnormal quality raw materials.  You may have a plan to reject any material that falls beyond the control limits established for that material.  This point will help drive the importance to your employees. *If your customers do not accept non-conformance, why should you?*  This will also help you identify any short comings with your suppliers.  Not all may be reporting the quality of their products.  You can request Certificates of Analysis to arrive with each shipment.  This will help ease the workload in your Quality Laboratory.  An occasional spot check to assure conformance will be easier to monitor.  Put the burden of quality on your suppliers.

# 106 QUALITY PERFORMANCE

If Quality is the moving target you are trying to hit, you need incremental feedback as you are firing, so you can continually adjust your aim. Your quality effort must be on-going and permanent. You need to monitor your process by using SPC and evaluate your progress so continuous improvement never stops.

# CHAPTER 5

## TASK TEAMS

The Webster's II Dictionary defines **TEAM** as a group organized to work together. **TEAMWORK** is defined as cooperative effort by the members of a group or team to achieve a common goal.

Two types of teams will be discussed in the next two chapters: **Task Teams** (Chapter 5) and **Improvement Teams** (Chapter 6). *Task Teams* are topic oriented and will reach completion of the task after a number of meetings. Improvement Teams can also be referred to as natural teams. These teams are on-going with a mission of continuous improvement. In this chapter, Task Teams will be detailed.

Task Team topics can originate from a Quality Suggestion or a Department Head request. The team topic is stated in the form of an objective giving the purpose of the task team. When you keep the objective in general terms rather than specifics, more ideas and good opportunities will open. If you state the team objective will be to cut the Widget manufacturing cost by $.03, the team will find a way to cut the cost by $.03 a Widget. But, if you state to improve the Widget manufacturing process, your savings may be far greater than $.03 per Widget.

Each team should have a Team Leader and a Team Facilitator. The **Leader**:

- conducts the meetings

- stimulates involvement from each member

- plans and follows through the agenda

- recruits volunteers for Recorder and Time
  keeper

- leads the discussion

- runs the meeting

- keeps the meeting on track

- makes assignments

-schedules the next meeting

- arranges the meeting location

A **Facilitator** attends the meetings to work with the team to provide assistance, direction, and support. The Facilitator also meets with the Steering Committee to share the team's progress and intermediate recommendations.

# TEAM LEADER SELECTION

The Quality Steering Committee or Quality Performance Department should carefully select the Leader for each team.  In addition to the SPC and Problem Solving Training, Leader Training may be required if this is the first time leading a team.  A section of Leader Training is included in this chapter. You will want to select someone that is knowledgeable about the topic, goal oriented, organized and works well with people.  Failure will occur if your Leader is not a team player, wants to grab all the credit for any successes, or does not organize the activities and assignments to be completed.  Good candidates for the Team Leader position would be production supervisors, group leaders, or a worker who is out-going and well respected by peers.

# TEAM MEMBER SELECTION

As with the Leader, the Steering Committee or Quality Performance Department should review who is invited to be a Team Member.  Select a good mix of employees who can contribute to the resolution of the objective.  Include people directly involved with the topic, an internal supplier(s), and if possible, an internal customer(s) of the topic.  Here is an example to better explain what the membership would look like.  The Task Team Topic is: ***"Improve the storage capacity of the Widget Warehouse."***  Members would be:

**Widget Warehouse Supervisor**
-Team Leader

**Warehouse Clerk**
- receiver

**Warehouse Shipper**
- loads / unloads trucks

**Widget Production Supervisor**
- "supplier"

**Accountant**
- inventory costs

**Customer Service Representative**
- "customer"

**Team Facilitator**

If you keep the membership from 5 to 10 members, it is a manageable team for both the

Leader and Facilitator.  **Team Members** should:

- attend meetings regularly

- help pick problems

- participate in discussions and make the meetings productive

- pay attention and avoid disruptive side conversations

- be open to and encourage the ideas of others

- not criticize

- help keep the meeting on track

- maintain a friendly and enthusiastic atmosphere in team activities

- treat everyone as equals during team meetings

- accept results of team votes and consensus

- collect data

- analyze the data

- recommend solutions

- implement solutions

- show thanks and appreciation to those outside the team who give assistance and help

- always strive for a win-win situation

In addition, two members should take on the roles of Timekeeper and Recorder. The *Timekeeper* helps monitor the meeting progress as outlined on the agenda, periodically reports the time to the group, and keeps the group on track. The *Recorder* documents the meeting activities, keeps notes of duty assignments, attendance, ideas, and progress. The Recorder also writes and issues minutes to the team members. The Timekeeper and Recorder can be either rotating positions among the team (excluding Leader and Facilitator), or be fixed or appointed by the Leader.

## TEAM LEADER TRAINING

This is a short training session designed to define teams, members roles, meeting steps and also to familiarize the Leader with statistical and problem solving tools. Leader training is necessary for a person who will be leading a team for the first time. Others who have previously lead a team may want to go through it again as a refresher course. A Facilitator typically is the conductor of the short course. If possible, it is the Facilitator who will be on the team with the Leader.

It is important that the team Leader not set communication barriers. A *communication barrier* can be:

- evaluating a member's idea
- implying wrongness
- showing superiority because of Leader role
- acting as a know-it-all
- manipulating or controlling members with own values
- showing lack of interest or concern to members comments

These barriers can be displayed in the tone of voice, word uses, and body language.

The team Leader should give the members' ideas precedence over own ideas. Do not let anyone be put on the defensive. Carefully listen to every comment and idea from team members making sure everyone gets involved. The team Leader should keep an upbeat attitude, be alert, and encourage humor as appropriate. Keep the meeting moving at a fast pace, not spending too long on any one step so boredom does not occur.

The *Team Leader* is responsible for:

1. **Planning before the meetings.**

- Prepare the agenda.

- Develop tentative objectives.

- Make sure the meeting room is reserved and necessary equipment or materials are available.

- Write a memo to the members about meeting date, time and place.

- Invite guests, brief them on what is expected.

2. **Conducting the meetings.**

- Provide an atmosphere for participation.

- Review the agenda.

- State objective(s) as needed.

- Lead the group through the problem solving process.

- Encourage participation.

- Handle conflict:

    - Recognize conflict
    - Allow constructive conflict to continue
    - Turn destructive conflict into constructive conflict (remain neutral;

paraphrase what people are saying; if emotional level gets too high, move the discussion to safer ground).

- Develop action plans.

- Summarize progress and action plan at the end of each meeting.

- Critique the meeting against your objectives:

     - What went well?
     - What can be improved?

- Plan for the next meeting (objectives, progress, guests, assignments).

## 3. **Follow-up**

- Make sure the work of the team is documented - *meeting minutes* (see **Figure 5-1**).

- Provide time and support for people to do what is expected.

- Keep supervision informed, bring back their comments.

The Facilitator will be available to help smooth out any rough edges.  After the first few meetings the new Team Leader will be experienced enough to easily follow through each meeting.

## TEAM MEETING STEPS

To have a successful team meeting, these five steps should be executed for each meeting:

1. **Purpose Defined**

A meeting may have one or more objectives.

```
┌─────────────────────────────────────────────┐
│ XYZ COMPANY                                   │
│          MEETING MINUTES                      │
│                                               │
│  Date: _____ Start Time: ____ End Time: ____ │
│  Team Name: _____ │
│  Team Leader: _____ │
│  Attendees: _____ │
│  _____ │
│  Items Discussed : _____ │
│  _____ │
│  _____ │
│  _____ │
│  Decisions & Accomplishments : _____ │
│  _____ │
│  _____ │
│  _____ │
│  Assignments : _____ │
│  _____ │
│  _____ │
│  _____ │
│  Next Meeting (Date, Time, Place) : _____  │
└─────────────────────────────────────────────┘
```

FIGURE 5-1 : MEETING MINUTES FORM

An objective is an end result or what the team wants to accomplish during that meeting. A meeting objective might be to generate a list of ideas, select an idea, or review data collected from a previous assignment. The objectives will collectively add up to the goal or purpose of the team.

For the first meeting the Leader should give an introduction of why everyone is part of the team and than state the purpose of this team. Select a name appropriate for the team. After the first meeting, the team will be identified by its name.

## 2. Agenda

The agenda answers the question of how the team will accomplish the purpose. This includes a list of the activities and time allocation to each activity. An example Agenda for the first meeting is shown in **Figure 5-2**.

Each member should receive a copy of the agenda *at least a day before the meeting*. This allows members to prepare for the meeting and make request changes to the agenda before the meeting. Everyone should receive a copy of the revised agenda before the meeting.

---

### THE WIDGET PACKAGING TASK TEAM

### AGENDA

| | TIME |
|---|---|
| 1. Define Purpose | 4 mins. |
| 2. Review Agenda | 3 mins. |
| 3. Select Recorder and Timekeeper | 3 mins. |
| 4. Develop Flow Chart of Process | 15 mins. |
| 5. Brainstorm Potential Problem Areas | 15 mins. |
| 6. Make Assignments | 4 mins. |
| 7. Evaluate Meeting | 3 mins. |
| 8. Schedule Next Meeting | 3 mins. |

---

FIGURE 5-2 : SAMPLE AGENDA OF FIRST TASK TEAM MEETING

### 3. Roles

The Leader should define responsibilities of **team members**, **recorder**, and **timekeeper**. Everyone is a team member. The Leader should decide before the first meeting if he or she wants to rotate the roles of Recorder and Timekeeper, or have two specific people keep this assignment each meeting. Then at the first team meeting designate these people accordingly. If the Recorder and Timekeeper roles rotate, follow through this step each meeting.

## 4. Execute the Agenda

Follow through the agenda making sure everyone has a chance to participate.

## 5. Evaluate

Successful teams evaluate how well the team achieved the purpose(s) and how the team can improve in subsequent team meetings. This is done at the end of the meeting with everyone's input. Each member briefly states how they feel the team meeting has progressed:

- Are we on track?
- Is everyone participating?
- Is everyone listening?
- Are we meeting our objectives?
- Where can we improve?

Try to hold team meetings to one hour. This will help maintain member alertness, participation and productivity. Special cases may require the meeting to be shorter or longer. Routinely, if a meeting is 30 minutes or less, it is not long enough to establish participation from all members. When longer than one hour, members may get bored, restless, or feel trapped into a never-ending situation.

As the team meets, the Facilitator will give updates to the Quality Performance Steering

Committee. Also, trials, expenditures, or major changes need the Steering Committee (or Quality Performance Manager) approval and the Facilitator can act as mediator between the task team and Steering Committee.

As the team meets, members are working towards a solution(s). An important factor in team decision making is having *consensus* by the members. Benefits of team consensus include:

1. High technical quality, since team members are experts about their own work area.

2. High commitment, since everyone is involved in the decision making process, and all team members agree to support the decision.

## TEAM RECOMMENDATIONS

When the team meets the objective it set out to accomplish, a formal presentation by the Team Leader should be made to the Quality Steering Committee. Before the presentation, a list of results and recommendations should be sent first to each team member for review. Then to each Steering Committee member inviting them to share any comments or questions they may have before the presentation. This can be a point where you may realize the team still needs to meet on an issue. Or, it can help you to prepare justifying your team actions enabling you to give an excellent presentation because all questions were addressed.

The Facilitator and Team Leader should *practice* the presentation to assure a smooth delivery. Leaders are not expected to be professional speakers. Doing a few dry-runs will help smooth out rough edges and make the Leader more comfortable with the speech and visual aids. Visual aids should always be used. They help stimulate interest. You want to sell the team's ideas. Seeing something rather than just hearing about it will help win the Steering Committee's understanding and vote of confidence. Make sure the visual aids are neat, pertain to the subject, and are referred to during your speech. They will not help if they are not used or are too messy to understand.

The task team members should be invited to the presentation to lend support. They can help address any questions which may come up during the speech. The Steering Committee may be able to approve some things at the presentation but do expect to have to follow-up with more information. The team should meet and discuss the comments and action items resulting from the presentation. Unless there was a major dispute with the Steering Committee, all action items and questions should be resolvable without another presentation.

A team recommendation may require a capital project which will not be completed for a time period after the team presentation. The Team Leader should make sure someone on the team is responsible for following the completion of the project. This team champion should update the Leader of any milestones.

The team may need to meet at intermittent intervals following the final recommendations to monitor the progress of implemented recommendations. Once success is achieved, the team should determine who is accountable for the new procedure, process, or equipment and turn it over to that party.

## TEAM CELEBRATION

After the team has completed the objective a team celebration is in order. The team should select what they want to do or receive within a budget guideline set by the Quality Steering Committee. The team also decides who is included in the celebration. It could be just the team, or expanded to include persons who assisted in getting information, running trials, or being a guest member at several team meetings. Here are some ideas for the team celebration:

1. **A group outing:**

- Lunch or dinner at a local restaurant or catered at their work place.

- A sport event (baseball, football, hockey).

- A trip to an amusement park.

- A picnic for the team.

## 2. **A single item:**

- A jacket with the team name on it

- An engraved pen

- Movie passes (2 tickets plus refreshment money)

- A calculator

- A t-shirt and hat with the team name on each

- A pocket knife

## 3. **Miscellaneous:**

- Allow employees to attend a seminar

- Give compensatory time off

- Let them be the "Boss" for a day

- Give them business cards and cases

- Give them personal stationery

Give each team member a certificate of his/her accomplishment (**Figure 5-3**).  Have each member's name done in calligraphy.  The President, Plant or

---

# XYZ COMPANY LOGO

## Quality Performance Program
### Task Team Certificate

**(Employees Full Name)**

**has made a significant contribution to improving the Quality and Productivity of our business by enthusiastically participating as a member of the Task Team**

**(Task Team Name)**

_____
President/Plant Manager

_____
Quality Performance Manager

_____
Team Facilitator

_____
Date

---

**FIGURE 5-3 :  TEAM MEMBER CERTIFICATE**

Store Manager should sign each certificate as a show of support for the team effort. You may also want to add the signatures of the Quality Steering Committee Chairman and the team Facilitator as an option. As mentioned earlier with the Q stickers, have a sticker to denote the completion of a team, such as a TT sticker (**Figure 5-4**). Have the sticker in a fluorescent color with white T's. Members can display their sticker on a hardhat, lunch pail, plaque, or locker. Don't forget to publicize the team accomplishments and membership. This can be done on a bulletin board notice and/or an article with a photo of the team in the company newspaper. Publicity helps stir interest in other employees to want to be on a team.

Task teams are topic related with an objective

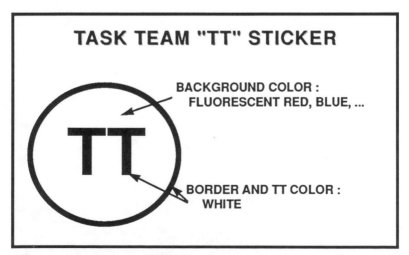

**TASK TEAM "TT" STICKER**

BACKGROUND COLOR :
FLUORESCENT RED, BLUE, ...

BORDER AND TT COLOR :
WHITE

**FIGURE 5-4 : A TASK TEAM "TT" STICKER FOR RECOGNITION**

(task) to accomplish. Improvement team goals are open ended, striving for continuous improvement. Chapter 6 defines what Improvement Teams are and what the differences are from Task Teams.

# CHAPTER 6

## IMPROVEMENT TEAMS

Task Teams were defined to specific topics with objectives to accomplish. **Improvement Teams** take every topic of a specific area, department, or product line into consideration for continuous improvement. Improvement Teams have *mission statements* directed towards on-going progress of an area (department or product line). Achievable goals are to be outlined so progress can be measured and the team can gain a feeling of accomplishment. Ambiguous goals may not be attained to the satisfaction of the team. You may lose team spirit as members become frustrated because they cannot clearly see the journey to the target. The team membership of an improvement team is the *natural work group*. This includes only the people involved in the particular work area. Non-related work groups can be included as team guests.

A task team objective is to be stated in general terms to allow ideas to flow pertaining to a specific topic. Since improvement teams are non-ending, you want to keep goals specific so milestones can be realized by the members. Your first goal of an improvement team might be to list every problem or thing each member does not like about the work area. If profits are down, that may be your starting point. A goal could state: *"We will increase the profit percentage 1/2% from our area by the end of 6 months."* In conjunction, a goal may be to improve the safety record by a given amount and specified time period.

## TEAM LEADER SELECTION

It is not as important to have the Quality Steering Committee input to select the group Leader as it is to have each Manager select the Leader of the area (department, product line). The Improvement Team Leader should be responsible for the area to be teamed. Do not select someone too removed from the area. It is best if it is someone who interacts with the employees in the area daily.

## TEAM MEMBER SELECTION

Team member selection will vary depending how many work shifts are involved:

### 1. ONE OR TWO SHIFTS

The members of the team should be all the employees from the area, if possible.  If it is a **2 shift** schedule, plan your meetings between the shifts (one half hour in both shifts if the meeting is to be one hour long). This will permit all the members to participate and feel like part of the improvement team.  If it is a **1 shift** schedule, you can plan your meetings when it fits your schedule best. This could be the first or last part of the day, after lunch, or after work (paying overtime).

When the work group is larger than ten to twelve people, you may consider having **rotating members.**  As an example, every six months three people will rotate with employees in the work area who have not been on the improvement team.  This will allow experienced people to always be on the team at any given time.  If you have 2 shifts, select the members from **each** shift so both are represented.  Include everyone in the area for distribution of the minutes to keep the group abreast of happenings or changes.

## 2. THREE OR FOUR SHIFTS

If the group works around the clock (three or four shift schedules), it is better to have members from **each shift** if everyone is not included as a member initially.  If your shifts rotate from week to week, you can plan the meetings to allow everyone to attend every other meeting.  To assure the attendance is above 4 to 5 members at each meeting, expand the maximum number of members to 14 to 16 people.

If the three or four shift schedule does not rotate you have several options for team meetings.  These can include:

- Have the Leader conduct two meetings each time (between shifts).

- Have the meetings scheduled to include employees for every other or every third meeting - receiving the minutes will allow all the members to be updated.

- Plan the meeting to include all the members, paying overtime as necessary (having people come on their off shift).

As in Chapter 5 with Task Teams, members should:

- attend meetings as often as possible

- review past meeting minutes before the meeting

- help pick problems

- participate in discussions and make the meetings productive

- pay attention and avoid disruptive side conversations

- be open to and encourage the ideas of others

- not criticize anyone

- help keep the meeting on track

- maintain a friendly and enthusiastic atmosphere in the team activities

- treat everyone as equals during team meetings

- accept results of team votes and consensus

- collect data

- analyze data

- recommend solutions

- be part of implementing the solutions

- show thanks and appreciation to those

outside the team who give assistance and help

- always strive for a win-win situation

As with Task Teams, two members will have to take on the roles of *Timekeeper* and *Recorder*. This can rotate from meeting to meeting, but needs to be assigned each meeting. Minutes distributed to all the members will help keep all members informed when not in attendance.

## FACILITATOR INVOLVEMENT

A Facilitator may need to be included as a member early in the team beginning to help get the improvement team started on track. Facilitators can also be used as *"consultants"* for teams. A Leader may want a Facilitator for statistical knowledge, to monitor the team progress, or as an advisor over a difficult circumstance. Otherwise, a Facilitator need not be present.

## PART OF THE JOB

Being an *Improvement Team Leader* or *Member* should be considered *part of ones job*. You are striving for continuous improvement through teamwork. Make everyone aware of how each person is necessary in the team and on the job. This awareness can be done by making sure results and information concerning the work area is shared with them.  Contributors will feel like part of the team.  A go-for person will feel like just that, a go-for.  When people have a broader view of their process, they will be able to see how important their function is in the process.  It will be easier to feel like being a member is part of ones job.

# IMPROVEMENT TEAM MEETINGS

Initially, you may need to meet weekly or biweekly to get everyone on board and starting to participate in the sharing of information.  The first few meetings will involve:

- flow diagraming
- brainstorming
- getting to know each other

Later, the meeting can run once per month or longer frequencies if waiting on results from trials on the process.

Improvement Teams should review and consider many areas for continuous improvement. Topics to consider:

- Safety
- Environmental Issues
- Quality
- Sales
- Employee Morale

- Housekeeping
- SPC Implementation
- Communication
- Yield
- Productivity
- Capacity

The Manager should work with the Leader to set a few goals for the team to work in achieving. Accomplished goals can be presented to the Quality Steering Committee along with a periodic status report.

## TEAM CELEBRATIONS

In addition to the presentation, make sure you have a celebration when significant goals are reached. Even though being part of the team should be part of ones job, recognizing good work with a celebration adds to that pat on the back of telling someone he or she is special and did a good job. Celebrations should be what the group wants within the budget guidelines (see Team Celebrations, Chapter 5, for some ideas).

## IMPROVEMENT TEAM STRUCTURE

Everyone in the company should be included on an Improvement Team, or have an opportunity to participate on an improvement team. **Figure 6-1** shows a diagram of how everyone will be included in a team.  Information will easily flow both upward and downward when sharing is praised as part of good teamwork, rather than ridiculed as individual mistakes.  *Improvement Teams are the mechanism for continuous improvement on a long term basis.*

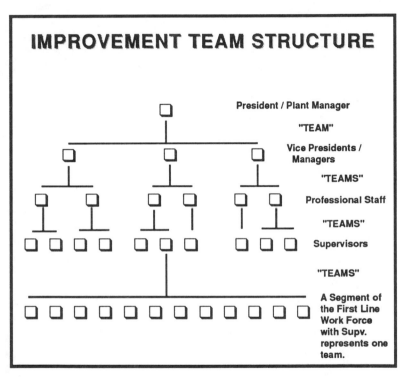

FIGURE 6-1 :  IMPROVEMENT TEAM STRUCTURE WITHIN THE ORGANIZATION

If it is worth doing,
it is worth doing RIGHT.

# CHAPTER 7

## SQC FOR CUSTOMERS

**A**s you make demands to receive quality products and service from your suppliers, so too do your customers expect the same from you. One way to go the extra step for your customer is offer to supply *Statistical Quality Control* data for your finished product quality to them. You can ask how often they would like to receive the charts, offer it to them with every shipment, or on a quarterly basis.

Providing you have a computer (a personal model will do) and printer, software packages are available which will automatically chart your entered data. Prices for these packages range from $500 to $1000. This software is simple, menu driven packages. One outlet for the statistical software is:

PQ Systems, Inc.
Box 10
Dayton, Ohio  45475-0010
Phone: 1-800-777-3020
Fax:  1-513-885-2252

**Figure 7-1** are sample charts from PQ Systems SQCpack software (price is approximately $950).

If you have Sales Representatives, make them aware of this feature of SQC charts to offer your customers.  You can show your customer: product consistency; process capability; or identify problems not related to your products (with other suppliers).  Sharing this information states to your customers that you are not hiding information.  Customers may be interested in other products you sell by merely seeing the statistical control capabilities.

To enhance this data, have pre-made folders to use in sending the charts.  Use the folder as a chance to advertise your company (see **Figure 7-2**).  Have a place to insert a business card.  The Quality Assurance Manager, Quality Performance Manager, or Chief Facilitator can be responsible for issuing these charts.  The sender should include his / her business card in the folder.  The customer may have a question about a chart or want to receive more charts.  The folder can also contain your company Quality Policy (Mission Statement) when you mail out the SQC data.  Include a cover letter to introduce your package.

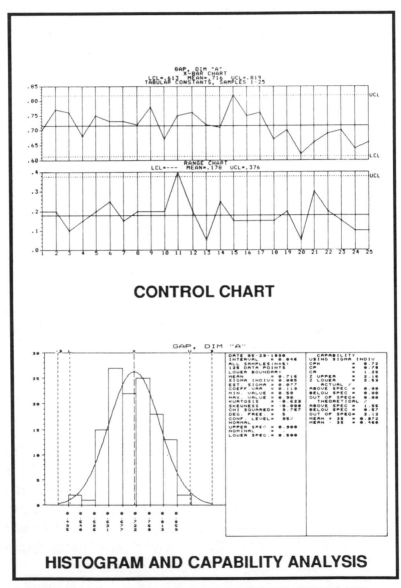

**CONTROL CHART**

**HISTOGRAM AND CAPABILITY ANALYSIS**

# FIGURE 7-1 : SQC CHART OUTPUT FROM PQ SYSTEMS (SQCpack SOFTWARE)

**FOLDER COVER FOR SQC CHARTS**

**QUALITY
FOR YOU
BY**

**XYZ COMPANY
"LOGO"**

**FIGURE 7-2 : A SAMPLE FOLDER COVER FOR CUSTOMER SQC CHARTS**

## AUDITS

Many customers are auditing their suppliers. They can range from a Self-Audit where you fill out a questionnaire and mail it back to the customer to an On-Sight Audit. For the On-Sight Audit, the customer comes to your location to audit and visit your location. Statistical Process Control and Statistical Quality Control are usually key issues with the audit.

Here is an example *audit questionnaire:*

## SECTION ONE :  YOUR COMPANY

1. Please give the names of the following:

>    Company / Plant / Store Manager
>
>    Sales Manager
>
>    Technical Manager
>
>    Quality Assurance Manager
>
>    Production Manager
>
>    Customer Service Representative

2. Who reports to the Quality Assurance Manager?

>    (Titles and quantity of people.)

3. Please supply:

>    An Organization Chart
>
>    Your Quality Plan
>
>    Your Quality Policy
>
>    Any Quality Improvement Plan you may have

Remarks:

## SECTION TWO : YOUR FACILITIES

1. Is your Company / Plant / Store layout acceptable?
   \_\_\_\_\_ Yes    \_\_\_\_\_ No

   If no, please explain.

2. Is the general housekeeping acceptable?
   \_\_\_\_\_ Yes    \_\_\_\_\_ No

3. Do you have an adequate Maintenance Staff for your location?
   \_\_\_\_\_ Yes    \_\_\_\_\_ No

4. Is your equipment adequately maintained?
   \_\_\_\_\_ Yes    \_\_\_\_\_ No

5. Do you have a preventative maintenance plan?
   \_\_\_\_\_ Yes    \_\_\_\_\_ No

Remarks:

## SECTION THREE : QUALITY ASSURANCE

1. Is there someone responsible for Quality Assurance on all shifts?
   \_\_\_\_\_ Yes    \_\_\_\_\_ No

2. Is your Quality Control System adequately documented (manual, test procedures)?
   \_\_\_\_\_ Yes    \_\_\_\_\_ No

3. Do you have adequate inspector training programs?
   _____ Yes   _____ No

4. Are there adequate training records?
   _____ Yes   _____ No

5. Are Quality Circles or Quality Teams in place?
   _____ Yes   _____ No

6. If YES to 5, what is the lowest level of membership?

7. Are process capability studies conducted where applicable?
   _____ Yes   _____ No

8. Will you submit a certification that the material or parts meet specification requirements?
   _____ Yes   _____ No

9. Do you operate a Quality Assurance System?
   _____ Yes   _____ No

Remarks:

## SECTION FOUR : INCOMING MATERIALS

1. Are raw materials coded and stored in an enclosed area?
   _____ Yes   _____ No

2. Are periodic spot checks made of raw materials from each supplier to determine compliance to specifications?

_____ Yes _____ No

3. Is there a Corrective Action Plan for suppliers not meeting standards?

_____ Yes _____ No

4. Are suppliers encouraged to use SPC?

_____ Yes _____ No

5. Does the supplier have facilities for testing raw materials on his own premises?

_____ Yes _____ No

6. Are adequate receiving inspection records maintained?

_____ Yes _____ No

7. Do you statistically chart raw material variables?

_____ Yes _____ No

Remarks:

## SECTION FIVE : PROCESS CONTROL

1. Are production operators and quality control personnel trained in Statistical Process Control?

_____ Yes _____ No

2. Do you utilize statistical methods for assuring product intermediates are produced within control limits?

_____ Yes  _____ No

3. Are process control charts being used as the product is produced?

_____ Yes  _____ No

4. Is statistical sampling used?

_____ Yes  _____ No

5. Do you inspect material at key points of your process on all shifts?

_____ Yes  _____ No

6. Are inspection and test equipment sufficient to verify in-process material conformance?

_____ Yes  _____ No

7. Do you maintain housekeeping in line with the product being produced?

_____ Yes  _____ No

8. Are work areas well lighted and large enough to allow efficient and effective implementation of process control?

_____ Yes  _____ No

Remarks:

## SECTION SIX : FINAL INSPECTION

1. Is final inspection performed by the Quality Control group?

   _____ Yes _____ No

3. Are formal sampling plans used and are they adequate?

   _____ Yes _____ No

4. Are written inspection instructions used and are they adequate?

   _____ Yes _____ No

5. Are customer specifications readily available and used at the final test?

   _____ Yes _____ No

6. Are adequate records maintained?

   _____ Yes _____ No

Remarks:

## SECTION SEVEN : PACKAGING

1. Are there written special packaging instructions as required by customer purchase orders?

   _____ Yes _____ No

2. Do your records indicate adequate inspection of the packaged material?

   _____ Yes _____ No

3. Are there adequate safeguards to prevent product from being packaged prior to inspection?

\_\_\_\_\_ Yes \_\_\_\_\_ No

4. Is stored product properly packaged to prevent physical and environmental damage?

\_\_\_\_\_ Yes \_\_\_\_\_ No

5. Do handling and packaging appear adequate to preserve product quality?

\_\_\_\_\_ Yes \_\_\_\_\_ No

6. Do you perform post packaged audits?

\_\_\_\_\_ Yes \_\_\_\_\_ No

Remarks:

## SECTION EIGHT : NON-CONFORMING MATERIAL

1. Is non-conforming material segregated at all stages?

\_\_\_\_\_ Yes \_\_\_\_\_ No

2. Is non-conforming material sufficiently identified?

\_\_\_\_\_ Yes \_\_\_\_\_ No

3. Are adequate records maintained?

\_\_\_\_\_ Yes \_\_\_\_\_ No

4. Do records show that reworked material is re-inspected?

\_\_\_\_\_ Yes \_\_\_\_\_ No

5. Is scrap material handled satisfactorily?

_____ Yes _____ No

Remarks:

## SECTION NINE : MISCELLANEOUS

1. Is there an adequate system for receiving orders, tools, and equipment?

_____ Yes _____ No

2. Is there an adequate system for receiving special requests from customers?

_____ Yes _____ No

3. Are specification records maintained which reflect an adequate history of changes?

_____ Yes _____ No

4. Is material identified with adequate controls throughout the entire process?

_____ Yes _____ No

5. Is your quality inspection equipment adequately maintained?

_____ Yes _____ No

6. Is there a calibration program for your quality inspection equipment?

_____ Yes _____ No

Remarks:

## OVERALL RATING

|  | Possible Score | Your Score |
|---|---|---|
| Section One<br>Your Company | 8 | _____ |
| Section Two<br>Facilities | 10 | _____ |
| Section Three<br>Quality Assurance | 18 | _____ |
| Section Four<br>Incoming Materials | 14 | _____ |
| Section Five<br>Process Control | 16 | _____ |
| Section Six<br>Final Inspection | 10 | _____ |
| Section Seven<br>Packaging | 12 | _____ |
| Section Eight<br>Non-conforming Material | 10 | _____ |
| Section Nine<br>Miscellaneous | 12 | _____ |
| **Total** | 110 | _____ |

If the audit is done on sight with the customer, treat it like a customer visit (Chapter 8). Determine how much time will be needed for the audit (ask the customer or your Sales Representative). Fill the remaining time with a tour of your facilities and presentations by key department representatives. In preparing the meeting room, have pertinent manuals, forms, samples, and charts available in the meeting room. This is an added ingredient to the audit - prepared and not shy to show your qualifications for passing the audit. *Do not bluff the customer.* Suspicion from the customer may lower your audit evaluation in all areas.

As you review the audit questionnaire with the customer, discuss realistic goals for any short comings which need improved to get a more favorable rating. You may find some areas requiring improvements that will take years rather than just weeks or months to implement. This is to be expected because of your budget restrictions.

Remember, be *honest, sincere,* and *prepared* for the on-sight audit. You will gain favorable respect from your customer even if every category is not complete. Change does not happen overnight. If you are working to make improvements for your customer, it will be recognized.

# CHAPTER 8

## CUSTOMER VISITS

**A** *customer visit* - - what a chance to show your customers what a winning team they buy from! However, if treated too lightly, it can be a ticket to failure. Every customer should be given the VIP attention. It can be scaled up or scaled down, but always the best you can deliver.

Usually, the initial contact with your customer is through your sales representative. He or she can help determine which customers would be beneficial for you to have visit your company. A benefit can be:

- selling more product or new products
- opening communications with your customer
- completing a customer audit
- forming a partnership for quality
- securing the business you have with your customer

You should consider forming a Customer Visit Team to assure that each visit is properly coordinated and followed through.

# GROUNDWORK

Your Sales Representative should lay the groundwork for the visit.  This includes preparing a history of the customer:

- Sales volume by product

- Complaints and contacts with the customer

- If you are to be audited, a copy of the audit form

- Details of their business (yearly report, number of employees, years in business, volume of sales, and any other significant information about the customer.

After determining that a customer visit is in order, the Sales Representative should contact the customer and extend the invitation to visit your company.  The customer may be first to initiate this visit.  More companies want to see first hand who they are buying from and openly seek these invitations.

When the invitation is made, clearly define the purpose of the visit.  The purpose can be:

1. Performing a customer audit.

2. Discussing problems the customer may be experiencing.

3. Forming a Quality Partnership, where some proprietary information is shared by each for the benefit of maximizing Quality Performance for the customer.

4. Exchanging information (quality, quantity, pricing, capacity, product lines).

5. Introducing a new customer to your business

6. Developing a new product for a customer

7. Getting to better know your customer.

8. Letting the customer see your process facilities.

This will ensure the proper people from both parties will be attending and that everyone can be properly prepared. To further assure a successful visit, prepare a *Customer Visit Checklist*. The Customer Visit Team can coordinate each visit with the specific needs of the customer by utilizing this checklist.

## CUSTOMER VISIT CHECKLIST

Customer: _____

Purpose of Visit: _____

Sponsor of Visit: _____

Date of Visit: _____

If an audit, has the audit form been received and completed? _____

Name and title of each guest:

_____

_____

_____

Method of transportation __ plane __ car __ other

Escort to meet at airport: _____ Yes _____ No

   Escort(s): _____

Arrival Time (and flight information) : _____

Departure Time (and flight information) : _____

Overnight lodging : _____ Yes _____ No

Dinner : _____ Yes _____ No

      Which restaurant? _____

      Number of Reservations: _____

Product(s) and volume we sell to this customer:

_____

_____

What topics do we want to discuss and name of topic speaker:

1. _____        2. _____

3. _____        4. _____

# CUSTOMER VISITS  155

Will there be a facility tour? _____ Yes _____ No
Who will conduct the tour? _____

Reserve meeting room: _____
Continental breakfast : _____Yes _____ No

Visual aids needed:
    Overhead projector _____
    Slide projector _____
    Flip chart _____
Number of tables needed: _____
Number of chairs needed: _____

Will there be a group photo taken? _____ Yes _____ No
Who will be the photographer? _____

Lunch: Catered _____ Yes _____ No
    Eating out at a restaurant : _____ Yes _____ No
    Number for lunch : _____

What company souvenirs will be given?
    _____ Hats
    _____ T-Shirts
    _____ Pen / Pencil Set

Did the Sales Representative supply the customer information? _____ Yes _____ No
Is the Agenda prepared? _____ Yes _____ No

Dry run for speeches: 1st _____ 2nd _____
Are copies of everyone's overheads submitted to the Customer Visit Team Coordinator? _____ Yes _____ No

# ATTENDEES

After deciding what the purpose of the visit will be, determine who should attend the meeting. Primary customer candidates to consider are:

- Purchasing Manager (the person who places the orders)

- Quality Manager (the person who aids in determining how the quality fits with their product line)

- Production Supervisor (the person responsible for using your products)

If the discussion will be technical in nature, invite someone from their technical staff. These are suggestions for the customer. They certainly will bring whomever they feel necessary to attend, or travel budget will allow. Remember, they should pay their travel expenses so as not to construe anything as a bribe.

The attendees from your company should include:

- The President or Plant / Store Manager
  This person should welcome the visitors and express how important the customer is to your company.

- The Production Manager
The process facility (via slide show) which produces the product for this customer can be shown and discussed by the Production Manager.  This person can also give a tour of the facility.

- The Quality Performance Manager
Your quality programs, your SPC efforts, and product SQC charts can be discussed and samples given as applicable by the Quality Performance Manager.

- The Sales and Marketing Manager
This manager can address specific needs of the customer and react if necessary.

- The Technical Manager
Any new innovations, computer systems, designs, packaging, and any changes to existing systems can be handled by the Technical Manager.

- The Sales Representative
This person is your liaison between you and the customer.  A successful visit will result if good communications are established with the representative and you customer.

# PREPARE THE AGENDA

Make this a prosperous visit for both you and

your customer by preparing a thorough agenda. This will assure no items are omitted. The Customer Visit Agenda should span the time period beginning when the guests arrive into the area through when they depart. A specific meeting agenda will be included as a subgroup in this visit agenda. Here is a sample customer visit agenda for a customer auditing the XYZ Company and arriving the evening before the meeting.

### Customer Visit Agenda

**Customer:** Containers Unlimited

**Purpose:** To discuss the audit form sent a month ago and to view our facilities.

**Sponsored by:** Marilyn Shove, XYZ Sales Representative

**Arrival:** Wednesday, November 13, 1991
      4:00 PM, Flight 123 on Fast Line Airlines
**Departure:** Thursday, November 14, 1991
      5:30 PM, Flight 456 on Fast Line Airlines

**Guests:** (Name and Title)

1. Matthew Marks, Production Manager
2. Marie Conner, Quality Assurance Manager
3. Richard Frank, Technical Manager
4. Brad Penn, Purchasing Manager

1. Escorts, Jonathon Davey and Lucy Young, meet the visitors at the airport in the company van.

   4:00PM

2. Short drive tour of the city.

   4:30PM-
   5:30PM

3. Check-in at the Elegant Hotel, allowing time to register and refresh before dinner.

   5:30PM-
   6:30PM

4. Escorts (Jonathon and Lucy) will meet guests at the hotel to drive to the restaurant.

   6:30PM

5. All invitees meet at LeFancy Restaurant Guest List:

   7:00PM

   **Containers Unlimited**
   Matthew Marks
   Marie Conner
   Richard Frank
   Brad Penn

   **XYZ Company**
   Joshua Michaels
      (Company Manager)
   Sue Juniors
      ( Sales and Marketing Manager)
   Jonathon Davey
      (Production Manager)
   Mark Celeste
      (Technical Manager)

Lucy Young
(Quality Performance Manager)
Marilyn Shove
(Sales Representative)

| | |
|---|---|
| 6. Cocktails | 7:00PM-<br>7:30PM |
| 7. Dinner | 7:30PM-<br>9:30PM |
| 8. Escorts (Jonathon and Lucy) drive guests back to the hotel. | 9:30PM |
| 9. Escorts meet guests at the hotel lobby for drive to XYZ Company. | 8:00AM |
| 10. Greet guests for a continental breakfast and social time in Meeting Room A. | 8:30AM-<br>9:00AM |

**Meeting Agenda**

| | |
|---|---|
| a. Welcome<br>(Joshua Michaels) | 9:00AM |
| b. Formal Introductions<br>(All) | 9:10AM |
| c. Slideshow of XYZ Company<br>(Jonathon Davey) | 9:25AM |
| d. Quality of XYZ Company<br>Assurance - Sue Juniors | 9:55AM |
| Performance - Lucy Young | 10:10AM |

| | |
|---|---|
| e. Break | 10:25AM |
| f. XYZ Company Technical Efforts (Mark Celeste) | 10:40AM |
| g. Facility Tour (Jonathon Davey) | 11:00AM |
| h. Lunch, catered | 12:00PM |
| i. Customer Audit (All) | 12:40AM |
| j. Group Photo | 1:25PM |
| k. Break | 1:30PM |
| l. Continue audit discussion (All) | 1:45PM |
| m. Discussion wrap-up / action items (All) | 3:00PM |
| n. Depart for airport | 3:30PM |

13. Escorts (Jonathon and Lucy) drive guests to the airport for departure.    3:30PM

14. Open discussion and review of customer visit.    3:45PM

## SET THE DATE

Review your calender.  Offer two or three visit dates for the customer to choose from.  Allow ample time for both parties to prepare for the visit.  Even if the date set is stated over the phone, send a memo to everyone, customer included, stating the visit date. Make sure you have facilities reserved for the meeting date.  Do not offer a date to meet and find out later that you have no where to go.  If you decide or must use an outside facility, make sure you review:

1. Is it reliable, have you used it before? You do not want to be cancelled at the last minute, or moved to another location less adequate. Your reputation is on the line with your customer if the meeting facility is not sufficient.

2. Check that you have enough comfortable chairs and table space. Commit in writing the number and style of each table and chair. It would be embarrassing to make everyone sit on cold metal fold-up chairs and the table top is even with your shoulders when sitting.

3. What equipment will you need? Will they supply:
   Slide Projector
   Projector Screen
   Overhead Projector
   Flip Charts and Marking Pens

   You may consider bringing this equipment along to assure it is in good working order.

4. Make specific plans for lunch. Will you have it catered or do you plan to eat in a restaurant? If time is critical, it may be time saving to have a catered lunch. This will save travel time.

Find out through your Sales Representative if overnight lodging will be necessary.  If so, offer to make the reservations.  Have someone pick the visitors up from the airport and escort them around the area.  This is a courteous gesture negating the need for maps and having your customer possibly getting lost.

If your visitors can arrive early the night before, plan a get-to-know-you dinner to welcome your guests.  Make reservations at a nice restaurant in your community.  Go somewhere that you or a co-worker has already gone and is familiar with the service and menu.  Invite enough people from your company to balance the guest list.  Keep this night social, building a friendship with your customer.  This will help establish open channels between you which will carry into your business dealings.

## THE MEETING

Following the *Meeting Agenda* on Pages 160-161:

Start with a continental breakfast.  This will save time so the visitors do not have to wait to be served at a restaurant.  It will also assure everyone has an opportunity to enjoy breakfast.  This can prevent everyone from being sluggish in the morning session, providing the choices are light and nutritious.

This time will also give everyone a chance to

re-meet and discuss the dinner the night before. Have someone state information about restrooms, phone facilities and who to contact with any questions on items such as incoming calls, faxes, or plane reservations. Have the President or Plant / Store Manager welcome the visitors. The purpose of the visit can be stated at this time along with a sincere welcome.

Allow everyone to formally introduce themselves. Each person can state name, title, and why he or she is there today. Then begin the program sharing information about your company. Focus these speeches on the purpose of the visit. If time permits, give a tour of your facility. A favorable impression will be made when your customer can see how clean your process area is and meet the people who make the product they purchase from you.

To save time, have a catered lunch brought in to the meeting room. Set it up in another room outside your meeting room to not disrupt any presentation.

Allow the afternoon for discussion by your customer. The morning presentation and tour may have provided many answers to their questions.

As a souvenir of the day, take a group photo. When developed, send everyone in the photo a copy of the picture. This will help serve as a remembrance of a pleasant trip to your company facility. Also give the visitors a company souvenir such as a ball cap, T-shirt, or pen / pencil set.  It will help to leave a smiling last impression with your visitors.

Make sure you allow time to wrap-up the discussion and list all action items to be done.  The Sales Representative should be the contact for both parties when items are completed.

After the visitors leave, evaluate the visit.  Was it successful?  Did you accomplish the purpose of the meeting?  What can be done better?  Were the visual aids easy to see?  Did everyone speak clearly?  Make sure the action items are assigned to the appropriate persons.  When are the action items due?  Should a formal report be written?  If an audit was conducted, what are your short-falls?

Mailing the group photo to each attendee will allow you to thank everyone for a pleasant visit.  Your Sales Representative should be following up on each action item to assure completeness.

A well planned customer visit should pay dividends in the way of knowledgeable discussions with the customer, more sales, less customer complaints, and a good impression of you in your customers mind.

# QUALITY -
# it is non-negotiable.

# APPENDIX I

## NAMES AND ADDRESSES

### Quality Posters

Vantage Communications
Box 546
Hyack, NY  10960
Phone:  914-358-0147

### Illustrated Paper

COPI-EZE Inc.
P.O. Box 64785
St. Paul, MN  55164
Phone:  1-800-843-0414
In MN:  612-636-3602

Idea Art
P.O. Box 291505
Nashville, TN  37229-1505
Phone:  1-800-433-2278

Memindex, Inc.
149 Carter Street, Box 139
Rochester, NY  14601
Phone:  716-342-7740

## Promotion Items

Best Impressions
348 North 30th Road
Box 800
LaSalle, IL  61301
Phone:  1-800-635-2378

Crestline Company, Inc.
22 West 21st Street
New York, NY  10010
Phone:  1-800-221-7797

Nelson Marketing, Inc.
210 Commerce Street
Oshkosh, WI  54901-0320
Phone:  1-800-722-5203
Fax:  414-236-7282

Rayod House, Inc.
P.O. Box 520 - QP
No. Arlington, NJ  07032

## Statistical Instruments

Quantum Company
Box 431
Clifton Park, NY  12065
Phone:  518-877-5236

## Calligraphy

Eileen M. Stephenson
Calligrapher
809 N. Grandview Avenue
McKeesport, PA  15132

## SQC Software

PQ Systems, Inc.
Box 10
Dayton, OH  45475-0010
Phone:  1-800-777-3020
Fax:  1-513-885-2252

## Quality Performance

Nancy Sue Mitchell, Publisher
QP Publishing
Box 18281
Pittsburgh, PA  15236-0281
Phone:  412-885-1982

# QUALITY each day keeps the competition away.

# APPENDIX II

## SYMBOLS

$d_2$      A divisor of R used to estimate the process standard deviation.

$D_3, D_4$      Multipliers of R used to calculate the lower and upper control limits for ranges.

k      The number of subgroups being used to calculate control limits.

LCL      The lower control limit ($LCL_X$, $LCL_R$)

n      The number of individuals in a subgroup, the subgroup sample size.

R      The subgroup range (in a sample size of one, n = 2 and R is the positive difference between two consecutive samples).

$\overline{R}$      The average range of a series of subgroups of constant size.

UCL      The upper control limit ($UCL_X$, $UCL_R$).

X      An individual value.

$\overline{X}$      The average of values in a subgroup.

# APPENDIX III

## INDEX OF FIGURES

# INDEX

# QUALITY products
# insures
# QUALITY CUSTOMERS.

# REQUEST FOR INFORMATION

So there you have the "How to" guide for implementing Quality Performance. I would enjoy hearing from you with success stories, quality slogans, any quality suggestions you would like to share, questions, ideas for improvements, areas not covered but you wish were included, *anything* dealing with Quality Performance.

Write to:

**Nancy Sue Mitchell**
**QP Publishing**
**Box 18281**
**Pittsburgh, PA  15235-0281**

I look forward to hearing from you.

- Nancy Sue Mitchell

# QUALITY PRODUCTS
# INSURE
# QUALITY CUSTOMERS

# ORDER FORM

Please send me _____ copies of **QUALITY PERFORMANCE - How to Implement Quality Awareness, Statistical Process Control, Task Teams, and Statistical Quality Control For Continuous Improvement in Your Organization** @ $39.95 each.

**Free Offer**: With this form (or a copy), you will receive a packet of the forms contained in this book .

Company Name: _____

Name: _____

Address: _____

City: _____ State: _____ Zip: _____

Phone: _____

Sales tax:
Please add 6% for books shipped to Pennsylvania addresses.
Shipping:
Book Rate: $2.50 for the first book and $1.00 for each additional book (Surface shipping may take three to four weeks).
Air Mail: $4.00

Please make checks payable to:
### QP Publishing

Mail to:

### QP Publishing
### Box 18281
### Pittsburgh, PA  15236-0281

I understand that I may return any books for a full refund - for any reason, no questions asked.